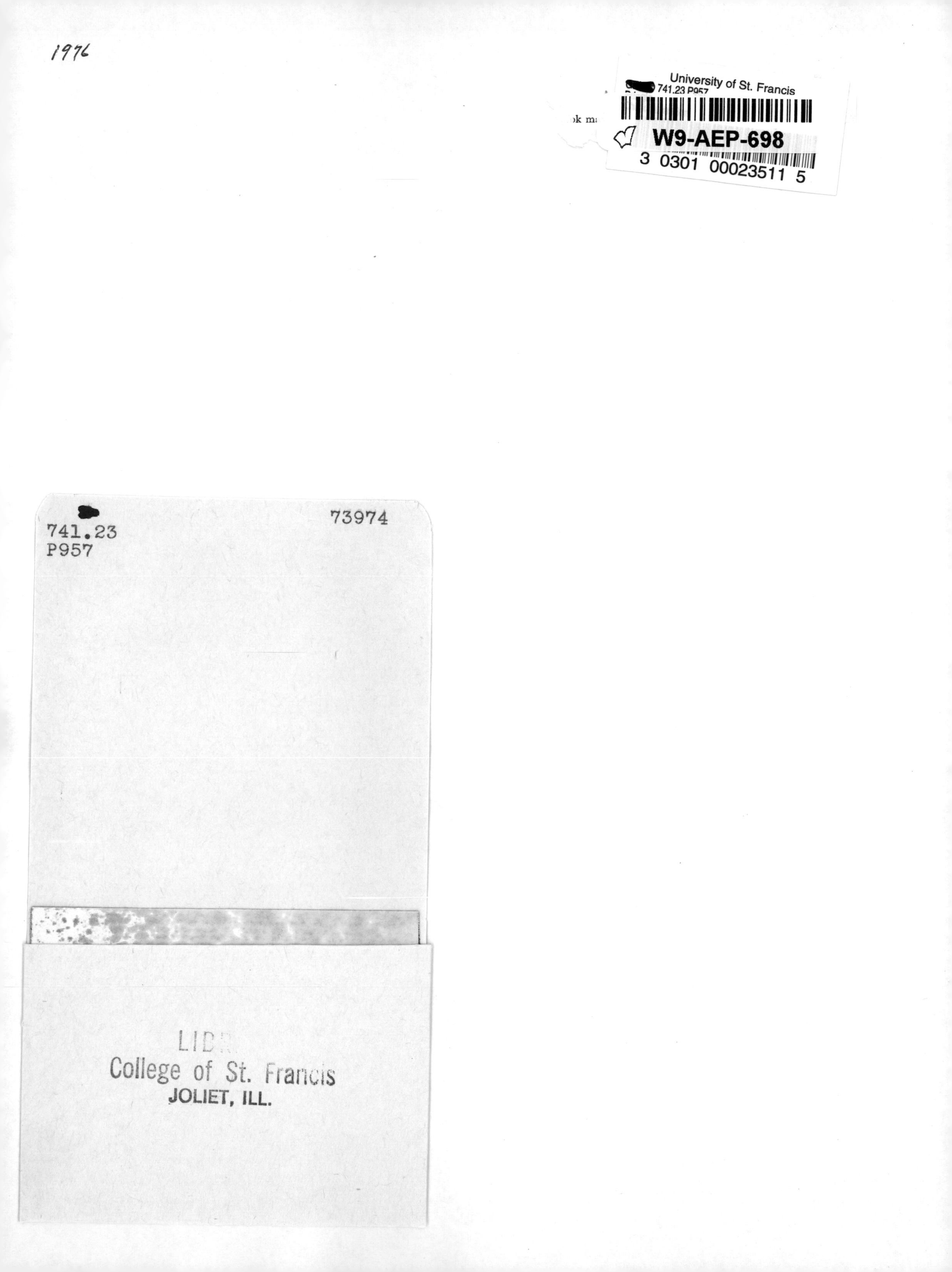

THE COMMONWEALTH AND INTERNATIONAL LIBRARY

Publisher
Robert Maxwell, M.C., M.P.

chalk illustration

chalk illustration

a manual for technical teachers

by B. PRINGLE

PERGAMON PRESS
Oxford · London · Edinburgh · New York · Toronto · Paris · Frankfurt

Pergamon Press Ltd., Headington Hill Hall, Oxford
4 & 5 Fitzroy Square, London, W.1

Pergamon Press (Scotland) Ltd., 2 & 3 Teviot Place, Edinburgh 1

Pergamon Press Inc., 44–01 21st Street, Long Island City, New York 11101

Pergamon of Canada Ltd., 6 Adelaide Street East, Toronto, Ontario

Pergamon Press S.A.R.L., 24 rue des Ecoles, Paris 5e

Pergamon Press GmbH, Kaiserstrasse 75, Frankfurt-am-Main

First edition 1966

Library of Congress Catalog Card No. 64-18837

Set in Univers 10/12 pt and Printed in Great Britain by
D. R. Hillman & Sons, Ltd., Frome

(1723/66)

preface

This book is intended primarily for self-help by young teachers and teachers in training who wish to improve their teaching ability by improving their illustration ability. It is hoped that the book will also prove useful to experienced teachers, instructors and lecturers, who know well the value of the personal illustration and also its difficulties.

Illustration, used here in the graphic sense, is one of the most important techniques to the teacher, and it is much more than the mere skill of putting an idea or fact into drawing form. To the teacher, illustration is firstly the selection of the most emphatic arrangement of content for his purpose, and secondly the rendering of this selection visually.

In order to emphasise both these aspects of illustration it was necessary to move a little way into the field of teaching method, but this has been kept to a minimum. The text has been kept simple, because the desired end is to be able to produce a teaching illustration, not a written examination answer on illustration.

contents

chalk illustration

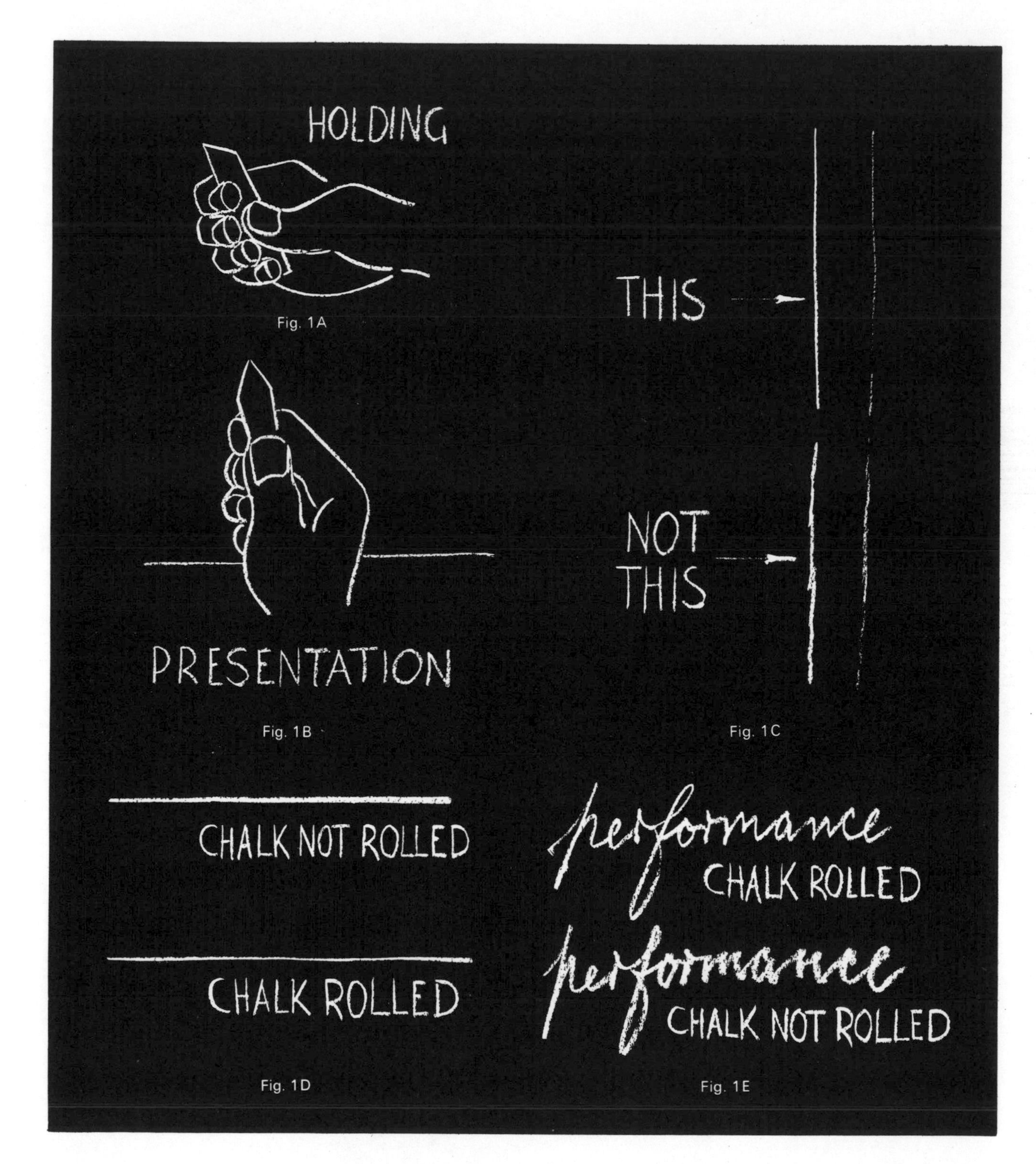

Fig. 1A

Fig. 1B

Fig. 1C

Fig. 1D

Fig. 1E

chalkwork 1

CHALK HOLDING

SOME GENERAL POINTS

1. The content of the illustration is more important in teaching than the execution, and how that content is used in the explanation is still more important.

2. The less conspicuous the execution is during a lesson the greater the impact of the content. Illustration is an aid to teaching, not an end in itself.

3. Pre-lesson practice pays good dividends.

4. A clean blackboard is a help.

CHALK HOLDING AND STROKE TECHNIQUE

1. Hold the chalk between the thumb and the fingers with the non-working end of the chalk pointing to the palm of the hand, Fig. 1A.

2. Present the chalk to the board at a low angle, Fig. 1B.

3. The fingers and thumb act as a chuck for holding the chalk, and do not contribute to forming the stroke shape.

4. The third and fourth finger-nails may be used as a steady on the board for special lines, but over-use of this practice will result in incomplete finger-nails.

5. The strokes must be firm not feathery, whether they be faint or heavy in intensity, Fig. 1C.

6. Develop the habit of slightly rotating the chalk as the stroke proceeds, and of changing to a new facet of the chalk face for a new stroke or word. This practice permits intensity without excessive thickness, and helps in achieving an evenness of work, Figs. 1D, 1E.

7. Always place the chalk length in line with the stroke being drawn, so that the chalk is pulled, unless you specifically require a broad line. This technique sometimes necessitates the wrist being placed in an awkward position. See Chalkwork 3, section 8.

Fig. 2A

Fig. 2B

Fig. 2C

Fig. 2D

chalkwork 2

STANCE AND MOVEMENT

STANCE	1	Stand back so that the elbow is only slightly bent, yet the reach to the board is easy.
	2	Start by working in front of the board. You will gradually learn to work without standing directly in front.
	3	Be comfortable, relaxed and balanced.
MOVEMENT	1	The stroke is made mainly through the shoulder-joint movement and to a lesser degree through the wrist, elbow and body movement.
	2	Use body sway to and fro to accommodate for differences of distance, Fig. 2A.
	3	Use side sway of the body to obtain horizontal reach, Fig. 2B.
	4	Do not hesitate to bend the knees for low reach in vertical strokes, Fig. 2C.
	5	Good balance is essential, Fig. 2D.

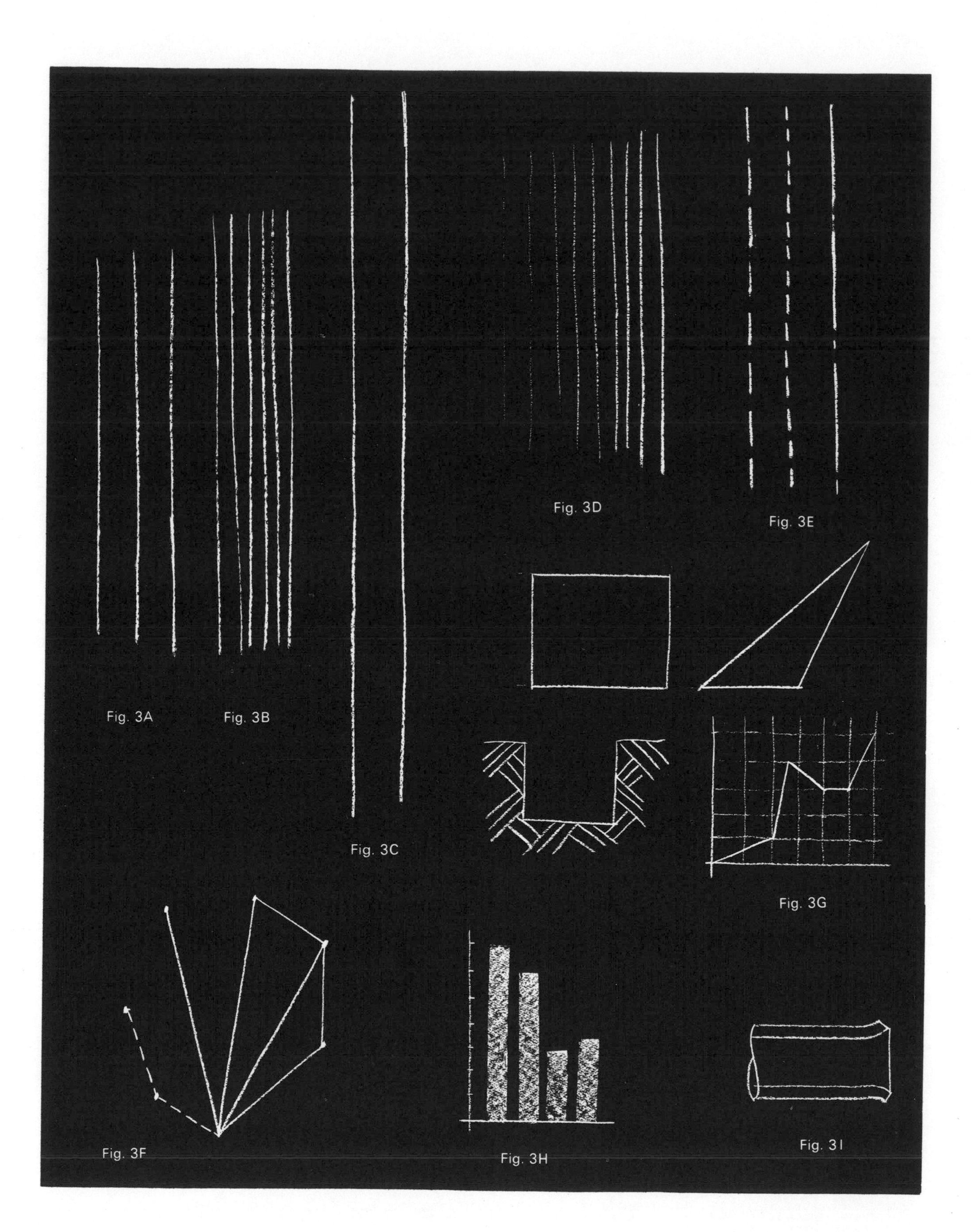

Fig. 3A Fig. 3B Fig. 3C Fig. 3D Fig. 3E Fig. 3F Fig. 3G Fig. 3H Fig. 3I

chalkwork 3

STRAIGHT STROKES

1 Start with vertical lines. Feel the simple up and down movement of the shoulder.

2 Draw some vertical lines of any length, Fig. 3A.

3 Try to place the strokes closer together, Fig. 3B.

4 Try to lengthen the strokes to the limits of your reach and bend, Fig. 3C.

5 Try an exercise of lines of varied intensity. Here you may use the third and fourth finger-nails as a steady, Fig. 3D.

6 Try an exercise in broken lines, Fig. 3E.

7 Repeat all the above exercises for horizontal strokes, keeping the chalk in line with the direction of the stroke to be made and pulling the chalk.

8 Repeat for diagonal strokes. It is here that awkward positioning of the wrist is sometimes necessary.

9 Try an exercise in joining points. The secret is to watch the point to which the chalk is moving after the stroke has been started, Fig. 3F.

10 Try plenty of examples of rectilinear shapes, Fig. 3G. It is useful to use very faint lines for the layout before lining in. These layout lines should be left in the completed diagram. Try to avoid the use of a board cleaner in this exercise.

11 Place the piece of chalk flatwise and draw some "mass" strokes which are sometimes required, Fig. 3H.

12 To draw two parallel lines close together two pieces of chalk may be held, when making the stroke. Try a few samples of holding more than one piece of chalk, Fig. 3I.

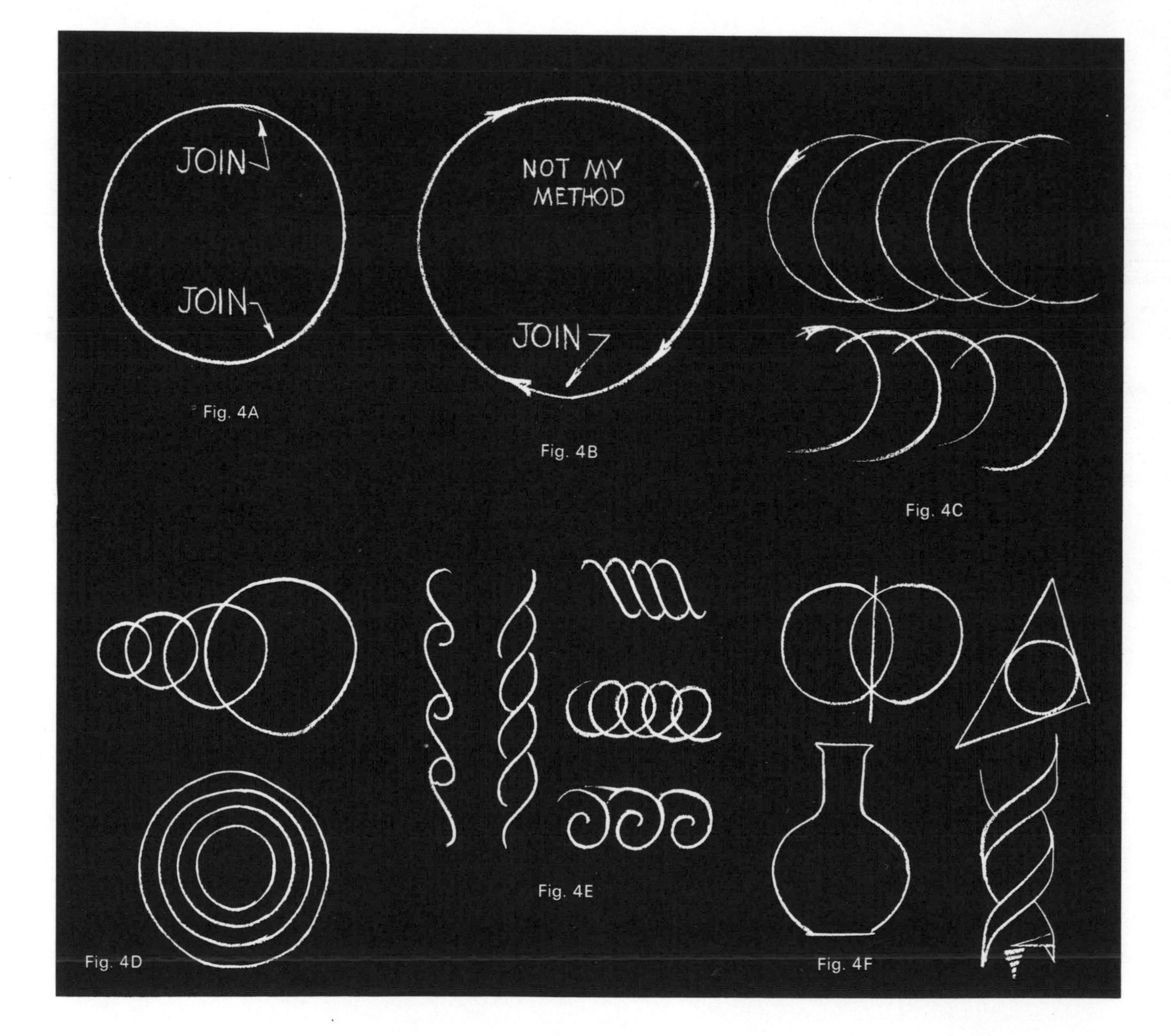

Fig. 4A

Fig. 4B

Fig. 4C

Fig. 4D

Fig. 4E

Fig. 4F

chalkwork 4

CURVED STROKES

1 Small circles are formed by wrist work, and larger ones by a combination of elbow and shoulder movement.

2 Do not try to mould these curved strokes bit by bit. They are bold strokes which are "felt" rather than constructed. To this end, it is useful, in the early stages of practice, to occasionally close your eyes when making the stroke.

3 The method which gives you the best result is the right one to develop.

4 Some people draw a free-hand circle in two parts overlapping at 1 o'clock, and 5 o'clock, Fig. 4A. Some people draw the circle in one continuous stroke, starting at 6 o'clock and moving first the elbow and then the shoulder to complete the revolution, Fig. 4B.

5 Try the stroke exercises in Fig. 4C and then plenty of circles of different sizes, experimenting to discover your personal method for the best results, Fig. 4D.

6 Try the free-curve exercises in Fig. 4E.

7 Try the exercises in Fig. 4F for combining straight strokes and curved strokes.

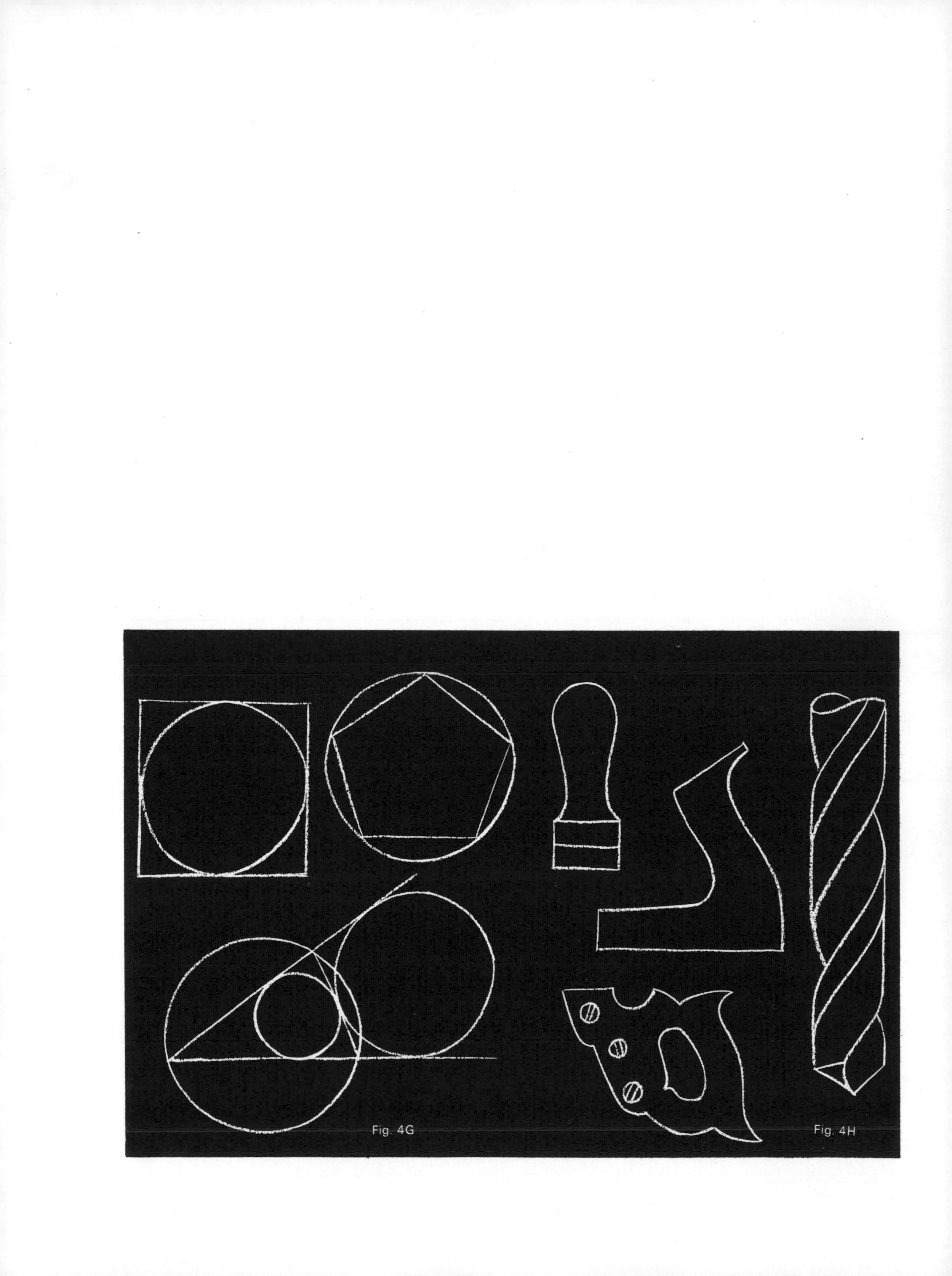

Fig. 4G

Fig. 4H

chalkwork 4

CURVED STROKES [continued]

8 Try the exercises shown in Fig. 4G for straight lines and circles. Make careful use of guide lines to achieve correct proportions and accurate placings.

9 Try the exercises shown in Fig. 4H for free curve strokes. Pay special attention to proportion and to quality of line work.

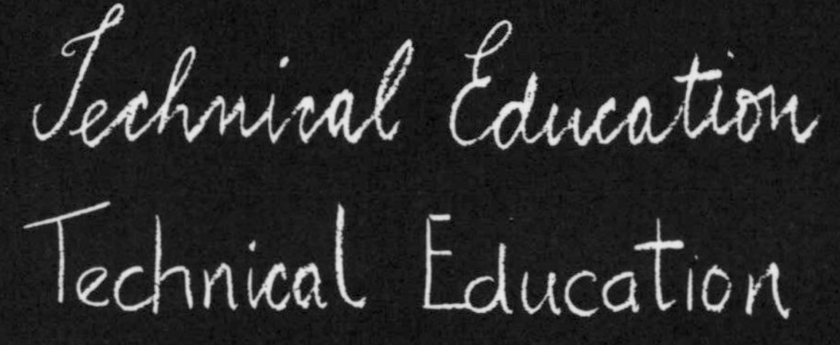

Technical Education
Technical Education

Fig. 5A

parallelogram
parallelogram

THIS
NOT THIS

Fig. 5C

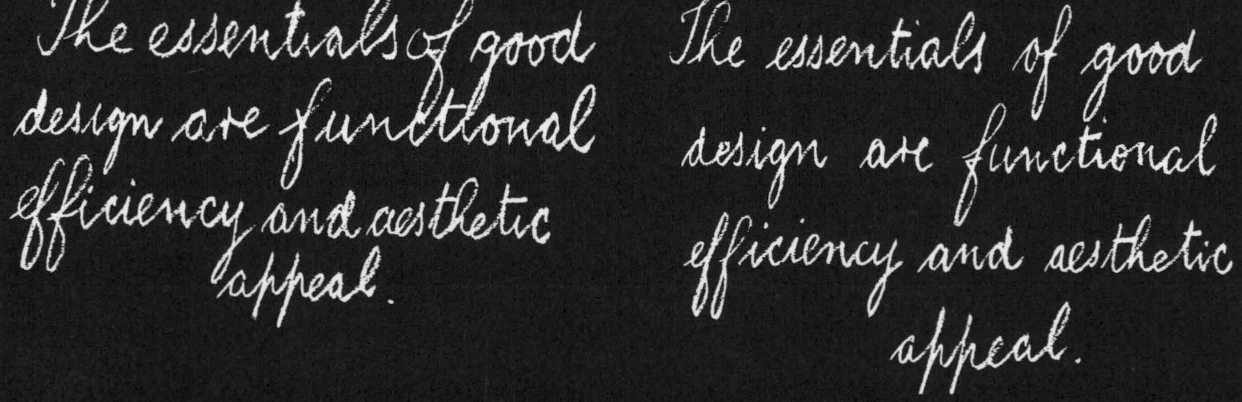

The essentials of good design are functional efficiency and aesthetic appeal.

The essentials of good design are functional efficiency and aesthetic appeal.

Fig. 5B

chalkwork 5

WRITING

The qualities required in blackboard writing are legibility and speed.

1 In developing legibility consider the following:

A **Style.**
Follow your present style first, but omit all trimmings, flourishes and mannerisms.

B **Letter shape.**
A full, rounded letter has much to commend it. Compare examples in Fig. 5A.

C **Size.**
This is governed by the chalk and the size of the class. Usual conditions require a size of $1'' \pm \frac{1}{4}''$. If the writing is too large it looks ungainly and is space wasting; if it is too small it is not functional. Check your work under the classroom conditions.

D **Spacing.**
This is a critical factor in legibility. Be generous in word spacing, even if you have to pack the letters. Compare examples in Fig. 5B.

E **Stroke thickness.**
It is important to get an intense stroke yet not a broad stroke. Keep changing the face of the chalk either by continuous oscillation or periodic change, and examine the working angle of the chalk, Fig. 5C.

F **Levelness of lines.**
If your writing tends to slope upwards as you proceed across the board, try putting spaced dots, one for each line of writing, on the right-hand edge of the board, and use these for targets.

2 Speed is essential for good co-ordination of blackboard work and oral exposition, but not at the price of legibility. "Little and often" is a good rule when compiling blackboard work.

Fig. 6A
Fig. 6F
Fig. 6B
Fig. 6E
Fig. 6C
Fig. 6D

chalkwork 6

PRINTING

1 Printing is slower than writing, but it embodies a greater clarity and an aesthetic appeal. Keep it, therefore, for conventional usage, for headings and for emphasis.

2 Develop a simple style of good form for both upper and lower case letters and for numerals. Practise the exercise in Fig. 6A.

3 Occasionally, for notices, a larger or a more ornate letter is required. Try the exercise in Fig. 6B about 4″ tall, with the thickness strokes added after each letter is formed. The advantages of this style are quickness and simplicity.

4 Sharpen the chalk to a chisel point and try Fig. 6C for single-stroke shapes and Fig. 6D for another form of large lettering. The same effect can be obtained by using a piece of chalk $\frac{3}{8}$″ long flatwise, for letters about 4″ tall.

5 Try double lettering by holding two pieces of chalk, Fig. 6E.

6 Teachers in the artistic trades should develop the technique of chalk lettering to a higher level than is shown here.

7 It is convenient to sharpen the chalk by rubbing on coarse glass-paper or on a cabinet-maker's rasp. The three shapes are shown in Fig. 6F. The single face "C" is most quickly sharpened, and is particularly useful in blackboard compasses.

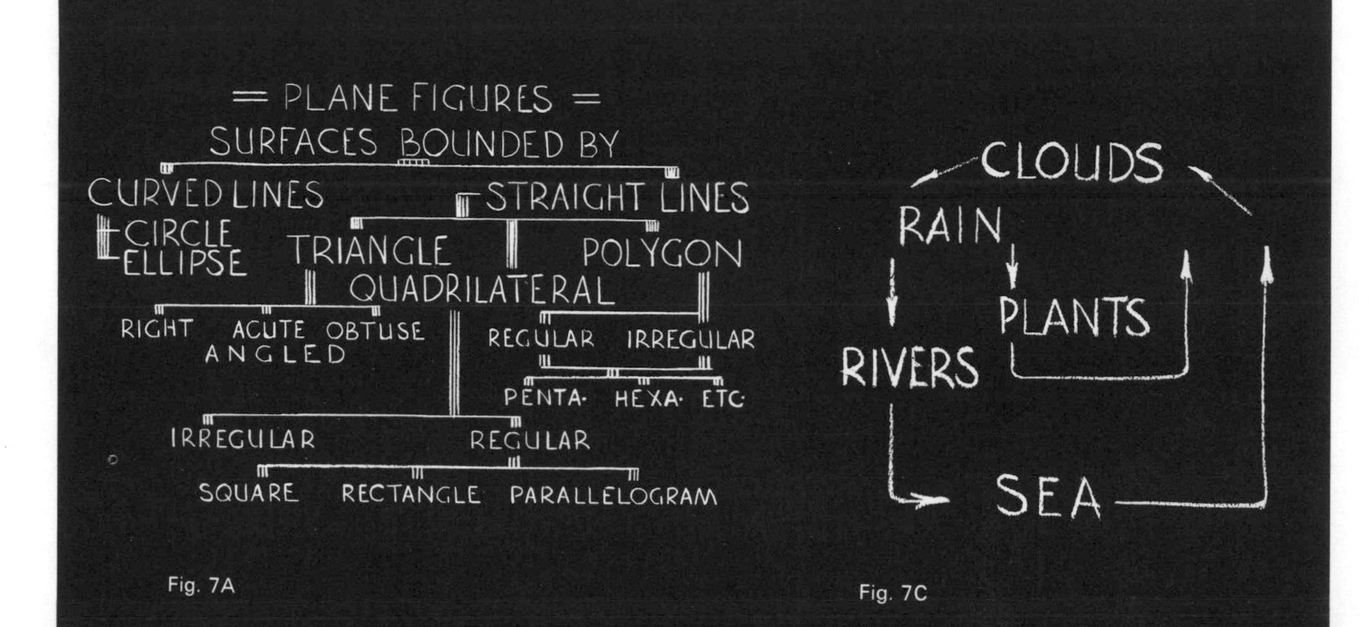

Fig. 7A

Fig. 7C

	HOT / COLD	TACKY / NON-TACKY	MOISTURE RESISTANCE	MOULD RESISTANCE	GAP FILLING	STRENGTH
ANIMAL	HOT	TACKY	LOW	LOW	LOW	VARIABLE
VEGETABLE STARCH	COLD	TACKY	LOW →	LOW	LOW	FAIR→GOOD
VEGETABLE PROTEIN	COLD	TACKY	FAIR	LOW	LOW	GOOD
CASEIN	COLD	NON-TACKY	GOOD	LOW	LOW	HIGH
SYNTHETIC RESINS	COLD	NON-TACKY	HIGH	HIGH	HIGH	VERY HIGH
RUBBER	COLD	TACKY	HIGH	HIGH	HIGH	HIGH
CELLULOSE	COLD	TACKY	HIGH	HIGH	HIGH	HIGH

ADHESIVES : COMPARISON OF PROPERTIES

Fig. 7B

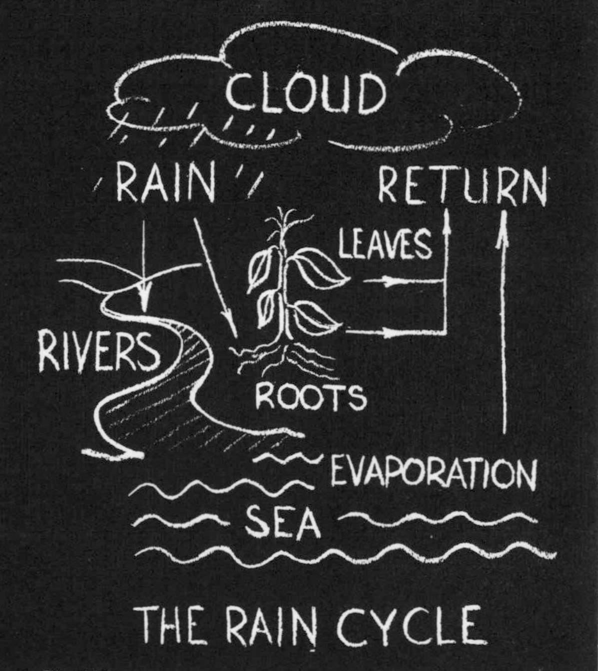

Fig. 7D

chalkwork 7

THE BLACKBOARD SUMMARY

The brief aim in giving a lesson is to make an impact on the class by personality, quality of material and clarity of explanation, and to leave a record for students' future references. A blackboard summary is perhaps the most used way of making the lesson record. It also helps in achieving the understanding by a visual appeal and by the lack of ambiguity.

THE BLACKBOARD SUMMARY

1 **Contributions.**

a) It forms a non-textbook record of the salient points of the lesson.
b) It forms a basis for student notes.
c) It clarifies and consolidates by appealing through the visual sense.
d) It offers an easy form of recapitulation.

2 **Qualities.**

a) It should be complete in its coverage.
b) It should be concise, because of time and space.
c) It should be well analysed.
d) It should be well set out to emphasise the analysis.

3 **Types of setting out.**

a) The Essay Form. This is not advocated. The duplicated sheet is better than the blackboard for this method of summarising.
b) The Note Form. This is the most used form of summary, and this sheet is an example. See also Fig. 8.
c) The Tree Form. Where there is an element of growth from a common source this type shows well the analysis. See Fig. 7A.
d) The Tabulation Form. See Fig. 7B.
e) The Cycle Form. Figures 7C and 7D show alternative arrangements of the rain cycle.

4 **Timing.**

a) The Prepared Summary. This is a summary which is complete when the class assembles. It is not widely used in teaching, but it is often used in instruction when a collection of data or directives is needed. Think out the merits of this type.
b) The Final Summary. This summary is compiled at the end of the lesson, often through recapitulation questions and answers. It is not very successful if the time span of oral teaching is more than ten minutes, because of the human ability to fail in receiving and retaining the spoken word. The final summary can be covered very well through individual information sheets.
c) The Progressive Summary. This summary is compiled as the lesson progresses. It fits conveniently into the lesson, it emphasises the particular fact under discussion, it is adjustable to the rate of class acceptance, and it offers a change in teacher activity.

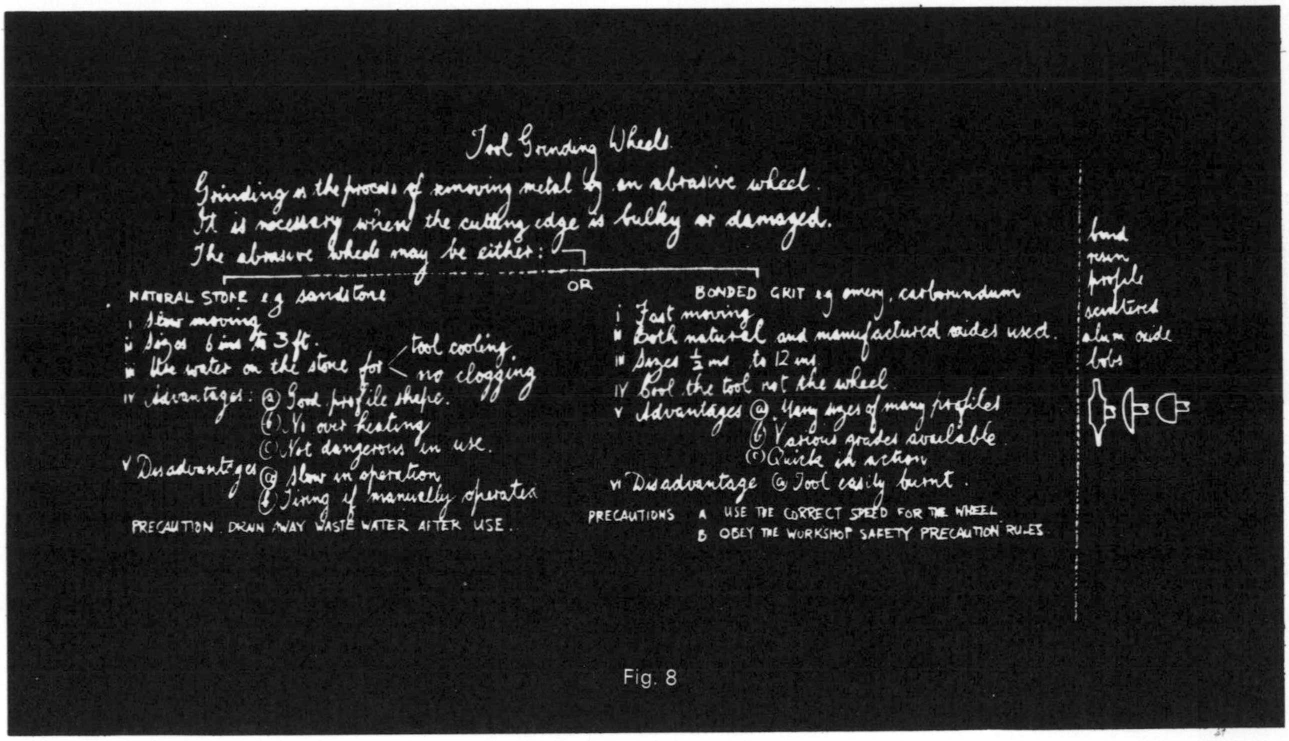

Fig. 8

The first quality desired from any chalk-board is area, and the roll type which allows a fabric chalking-area to be changed has this advantage, although the whole area is not uncovered at any one time. The teacher should ensure that he has a functional minimum of board space and then he should plan to work efficiently inside this space. Ancillary boards are simple to make, but excessive board area can work against clever planning and setting out.

Remember firstly, that it is not the type of board surface which matters, but the quality of illustration placed upon the surface, and secondly, that the blackboard work is an aid to teaching, not an end in itself.

chalkwork 8

USING THE BLACKBOARD

1 Make sure that the board is completely clean before you start and leave the board clean when you finish. To have the board partially filled with some other work will detract from your lesson impact. The board cleaner will leave a cleaner surface on a wooden board if used along the grain.

2 Know the placing and the arrangement of the content before the lesson starts. A pre-lesson practice is valuable, and, if desired, faint location dots may be left on the blackboard for the control of the arrangement.

3 Use the top quarter of the board. Many teachers waste this space which is usually needed later in the lesson.

4 Keep incidental work separate from the main record. It is convenient to place it in a column at the right-hand side. See Fig. 8.

5 Emphasise the importance of the points by their placing and spacing in the layout, Fig. 8.

6 If the topic is large, clean the board at chosen intervals, not when the board happens to become full. Each interval will offer an appropriate stage for revision, for reviewing, for discussion and for class recording if desired.

7 Ancillary boards 3′ × 2′ are very helpful where prepared work is required.

8 New, unfamiliar or important terms must be given special consideration. This may be achieved by increasing the size, increasing the spacing, changing to printing, or using colour.

9 All colour work and shading must be purposeful. See Chalkwork 13, page 35.

10 A monthly wash and a termly coat of renovator for the board will help in clarity.

11 The common materials for chalk-boards are timber, plywood, composite board, roughened glass, slate and supported fabric for the roll type. Roughened glass gives the most attractive working surface, slate often develops slippery patches, and timber has many grain pores which collect dust and produce a greyish appearance. In spite of the disadvantage, plywood perhaps offers the best compromise, because of its cheapness, its easy renovation and its adaptability to extension in fixed or portable forms.

continued opposite

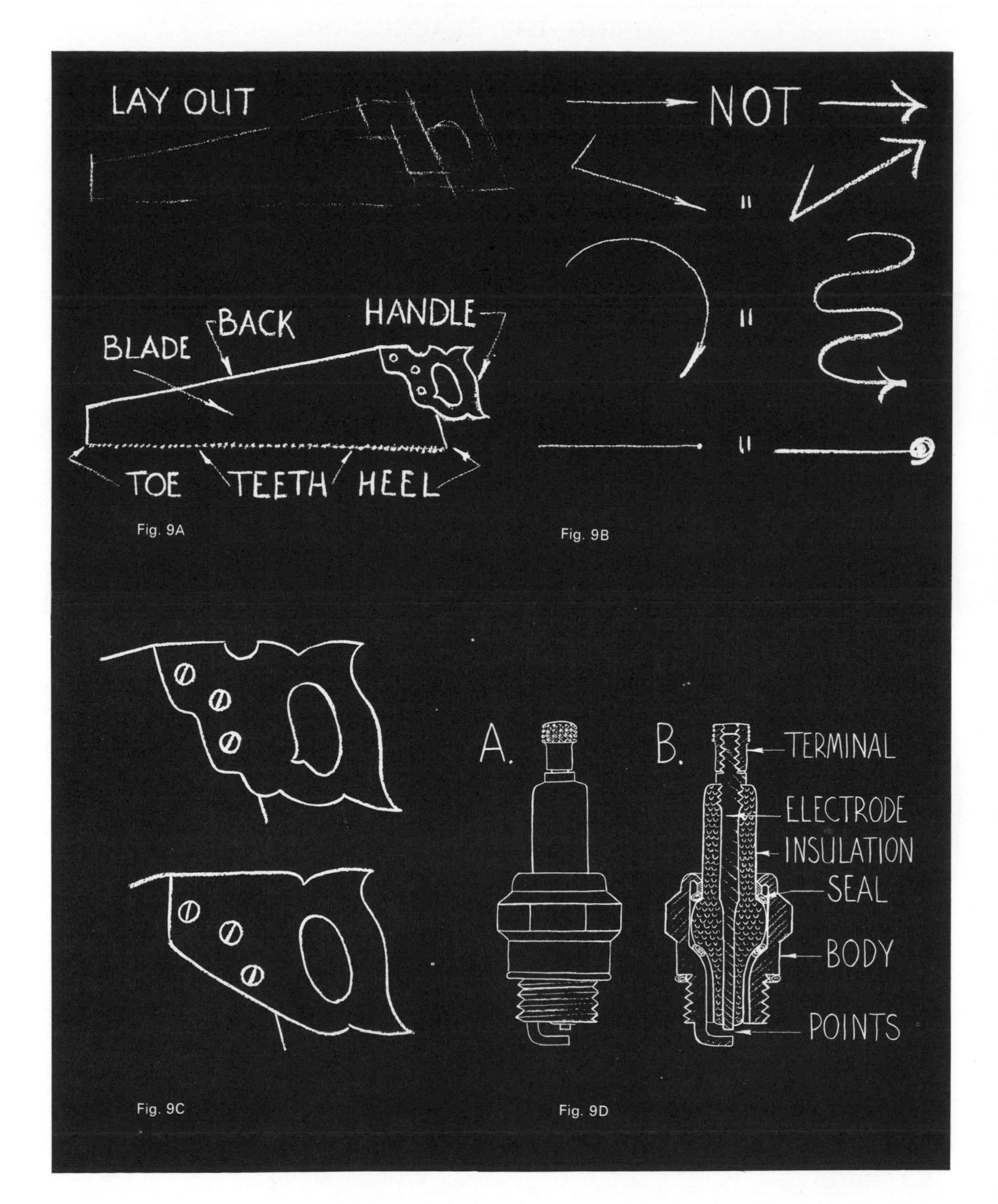

Fig. 9A

Fig. 9B

Fig. 9C

Fig. 9D

chalkwork 9

THE BLACKBOARD DIAGRAM

1 A diagram, or a collection of diagrams, may be incidental, i.e. arising at any time to clarify a point; it may be an essential part of the lesson record in conjunction with some written work; or it may be a complete lesson record in itself. The comments on Contributions and Qualities made on the Written Summary, Chalkwork 7, apply equally well to a diagram summary.

2 The way the diagram is used in the exposition is of paramount importance and the progressive diagram, i.e. the diagram which grows as the lesson develops, has the greatest impact value. Complexity of diagram and lack of skill often deter a teacher from using this type, and he uses a prepared diagram instead. See Prepared Work and Charts 1, page 39.

3 **Making a Diagram.**

a) Use light layout lines or guide strokes first. These lines, which are left in the finished diagram, allow the proportions to be estimated and the placings achieved, Fig. 9A.

b) Use bold, clean strokes for final lines.

c) Label the diagram with neat lettering and accurate connecting arrows, Fig. 9A and Fig. 9B. Figures 9D, 12 and 15I show other methods of labelling.

d) Use colour as desired for emphasis, clarity and conventional practice. See Chalkwork 13, page 35.

e) Do not try to be photographic, but simplify and symbolise to the needs of the situation. Figure 9C shows two forms of a saw handle, one photographic and one simplified.

f) The diagram must give the most information in the clearest manner. This means that the correct selection of the material is the first essential, the arrangement is the second essential and the execution is the third essential. In Fig. 9D of a sparking plug, the diagram A lacks the information of diagram B.

g) If there are several diagrams, spacing is very important. Refer to Chalkwork 5, spacing of writing, page 13. Keep good spacing between the diagrams to avoid confusion.

h) In making teaching diagrams, remember that you often have a duty to help the student to reproduce the diagram for examination purposes. Therefore keep to essential principles and use the simplest forms. If the teacher cannot create the diagram on the blackboard, it is unfair to expect a student to produce that diagram in an examination.

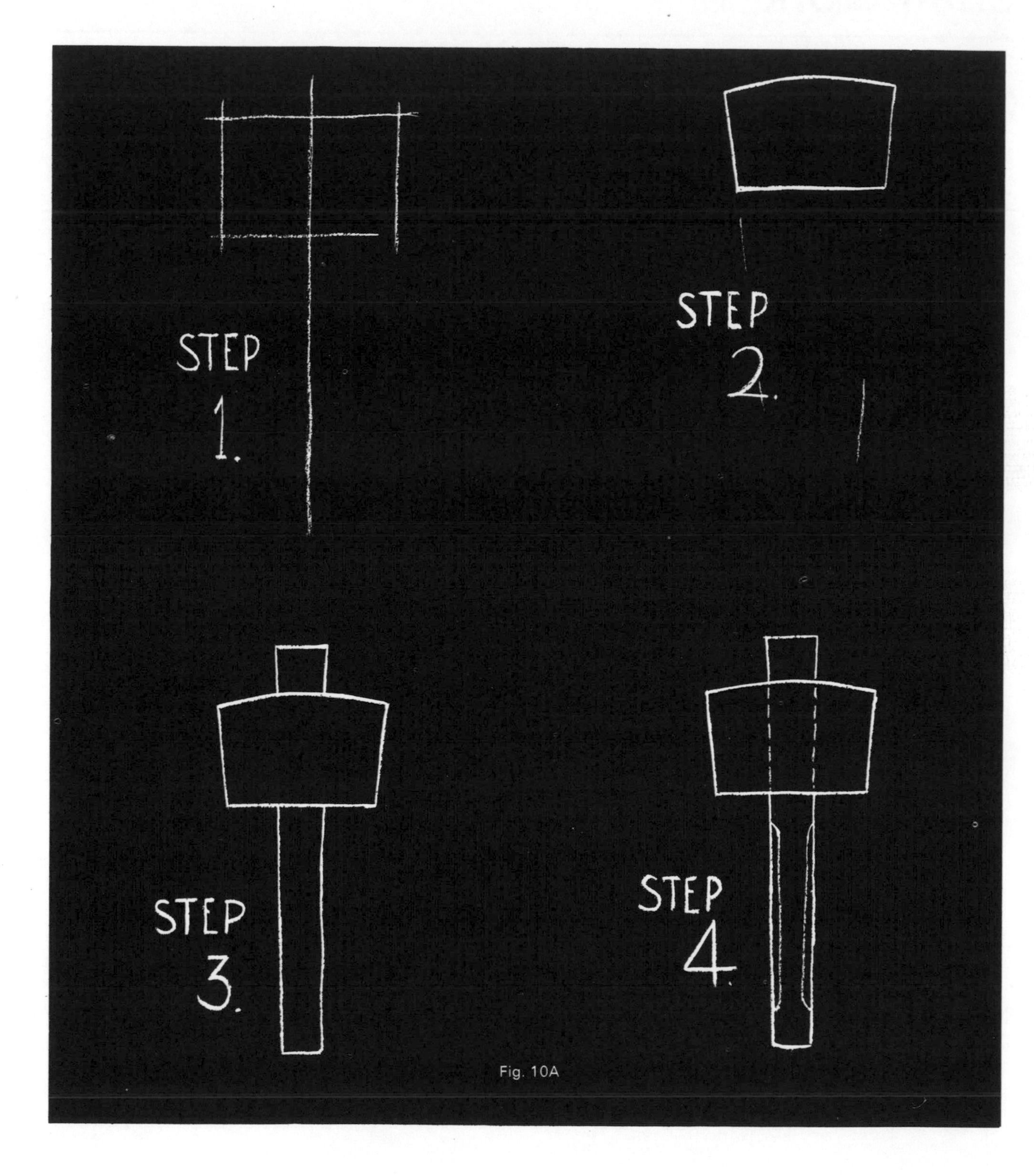

Fig. 10A

chalkwork 10

THE PROGRESSIVE DIAGRAM

1 This type of diagram is developed as the lesson proceeds, and it is so valuable in teaching that every teacher should acquire the skill to make an apparently difficult diagram concurrently with his exposition. The progressive diagram can be controlled to fit the rate of presentation; it offers a working from the simple to the complex; it focuses the attention on the individual point under discussion; it incorporates only the material selected for the lesson; and it shows the student how the diagram may be produced.

2 **Hints.**

a) Know your material.
b) Know the proportions.
c) Know the spacings.
d) Work from essential principles or features.
e) Work in short spells to give a balance of chalk and talk.
f) Do not expect to do impromptu work. Pre-thinking and pre-practice are part of lesson preparation and are vitally necessary.

chalkwork 10A

Constructing the Progressive Diagram. Example: A Mallet.

1 Lightly sketch out the essentials, Fig. 10A, step 1.

2 Develop the head, letting the shape grow according to the technical details expounded, Fig. 10A, step 2.

3 Draw in the general shape of the handle, letting the shape arise from the qualities described, Fig. 10A, step 3.

4 Add the final details and complete the diagram, Fig. 10A, step 4. No mention of labels has been made in this first exercise, for the sake of simplicity.

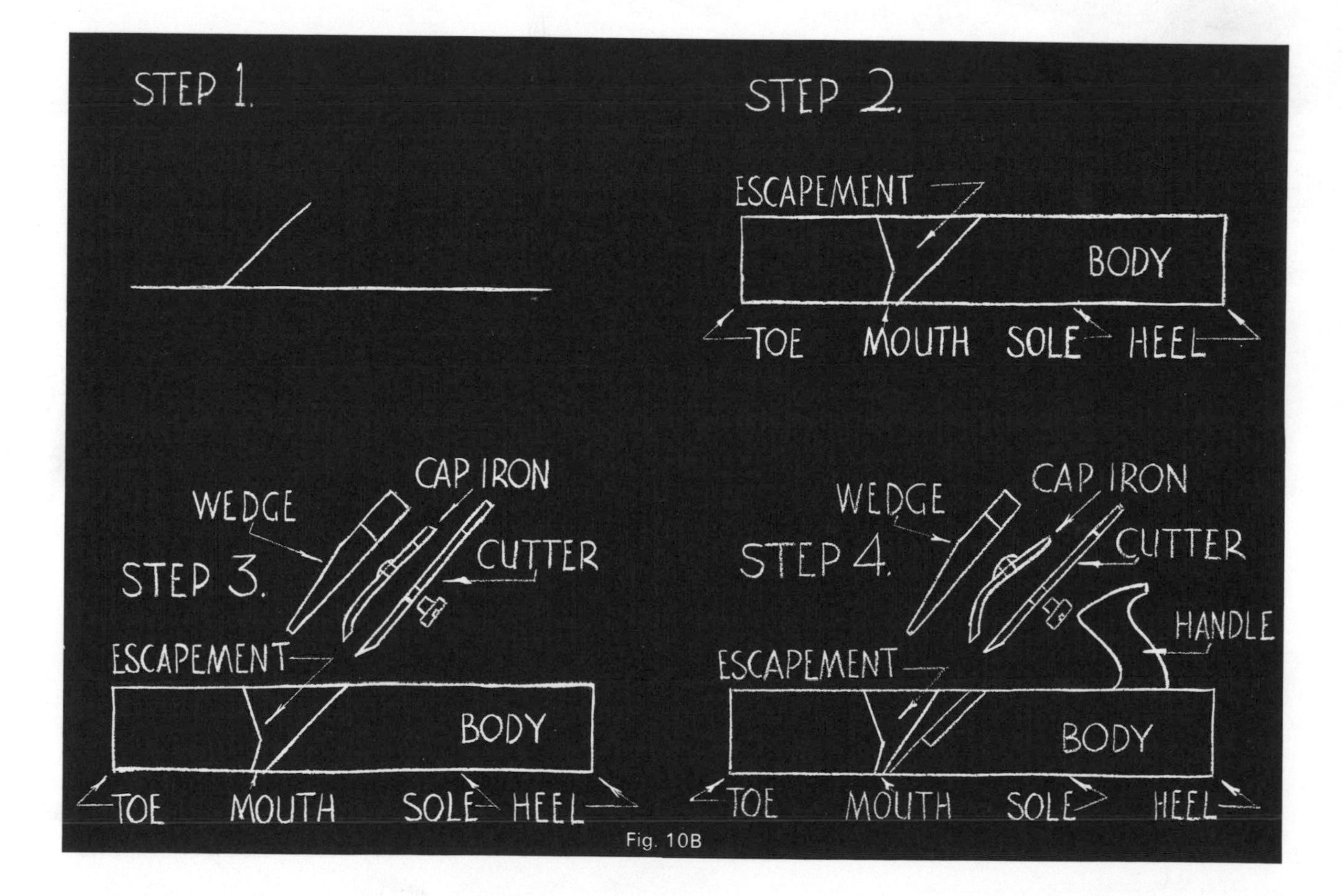
STEP 1.
STEP 2.
ESCAPEMENT
BODY
TOE
MOUTH
SOLE
HEEL
CAP IRON
WEDGE
CUTTER
STEP 3.
ESCAPEMENT
BODY
TOE
MOUTH
SOLE
HEEL
WEDGE
CAP IRON
CUTTER
STEP 4.
HANDLE
ESCAPEMENT
BODY
TOE
MOUTH
SOLE
HEEL
Fig. 10B

chalkwork 10B

Constructing the Progressive Diagram. Example: A Wooden Jack-plane. Work from the basic qualities, adding detail and refinement as the tool is developed.

1 A cutter and a true base constitute any plane. Start with these for Fig. 10B, step 1.

2 The base must be the base of a body. Add the body details and label as these are expounded, Fig. 10B, step 2.

3 Develop the cutter assembly and add the labels, Fig. 10B, step 3.

4 Complete the diagram with the housing for the cutter assembly and the handle for efficient usage, Fig. 10B, step 4.

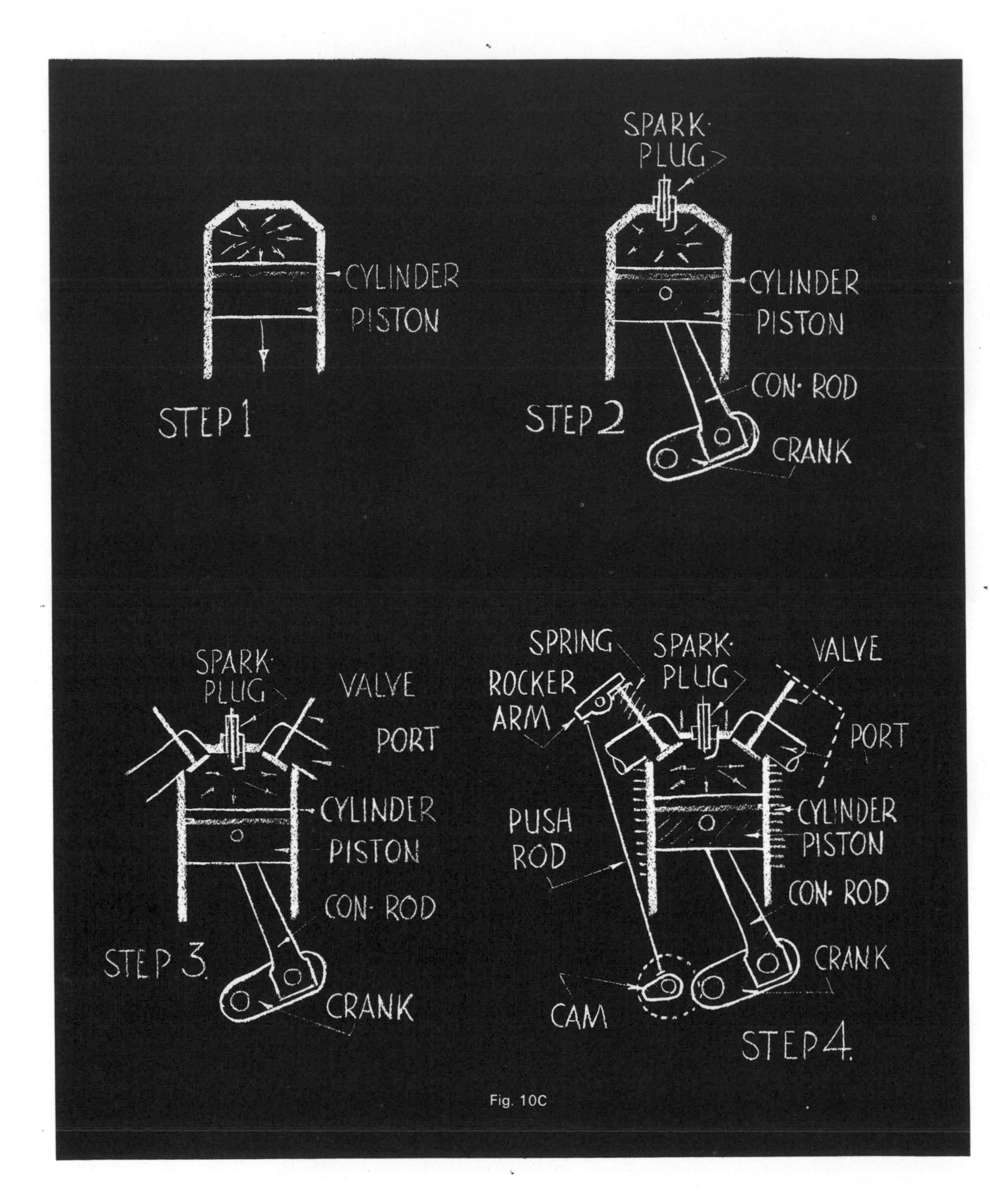
CYLINDER
PISTON
STEP 1
SPARK·
PLUG
CYLINDER
PISTON
CON· ROD
STEP 2
CRANK
SPARK·
PLUG
VALVE
PORT
CYLINDER
PISTON
CON· ROD
STEP 3.
CRANK
SPRING
SPARK·
PLUG
VALVE
ROCKER
ARM
PORT
PUSH
ROD
CYLINDER
PISTON
CON· ROD
CRANK
CAM
STEP 4.
Fig. 10C

chalkwork 10C

Constructing the Progressive Diagram. Example: The Four-stroke I.C. Engine. Work from basic principles adding detail according to the working needs.

1 Lightly sketch out a rectangle for the cylinder.

2 Draw in the cylinder, the piston and the burning gases, as the idea of expansion and force is established. The chalk is used broadside for the cylinder, Fig. 10C, step 1.

3 Develop the concept of the change from reciprocation to rotation, and draw in the crank, the connecting rod, and the bearings, adding the labels. Deal with the basic idea of a spark plug, then add this component to the drawing, Fig. 10C, step 2.

4 The next need is to get the mixture into and out of the cylinder. Develop this problem, adding the ports and valves. (The valve area is made by rubbing out small breaks in the drawing of step 2.) Fig. 10C, Step 3.

5 Proceed to the idea that the valves are normally closed. Add the valve springs and label the same. Develop the rocker arm and continue to the cam and push rod. Add the labels. A brief coverage of the four strokes will permit the cam drive to be placed in, and then the cooling fins are added. Fig. 10C, step 4, is the diagram completed.

This looks a difficult diagram to build concurrently with the teaching, but it will grow easily if taken slowly, in small steps co-ordinated with the exposition.

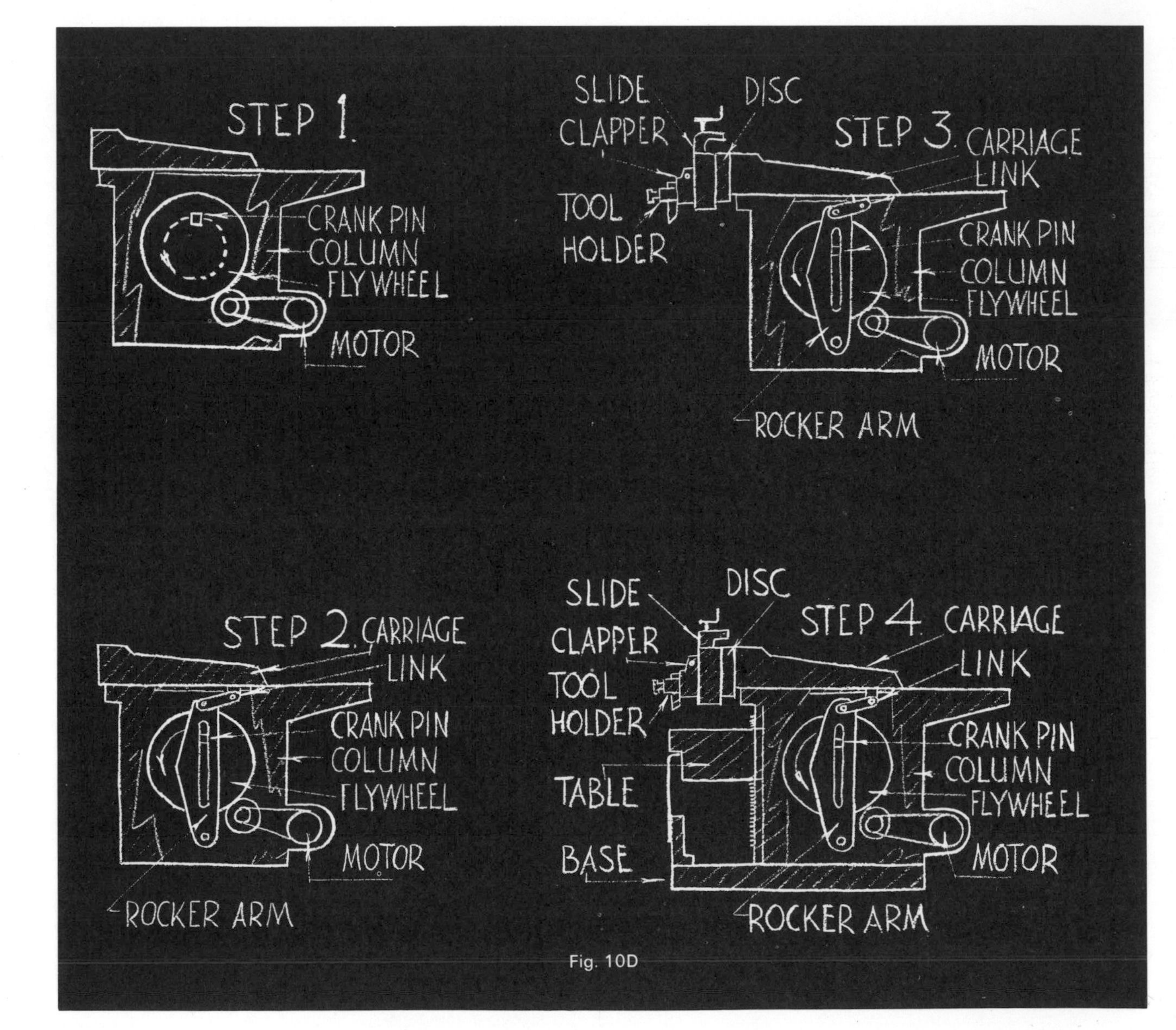
STEP 1.
CRANK PIN
COLUMN
FLY WHEEL
MOTOR
SLIDE
DISC
CLAPPER
TOOL
HOLDER
STEP 3.
CARRIAGE
LINK
CRANK PIN
COLUMN
FLYWHEEL
MOTOR
ROCKER ARM
STEP 2.
CARRIAGE
LINK
CRANK PIN
COLUMN
FLYWHEEL
MOTOR
ROCKER ARM
SLIDE
DISC
CLAPPER
TOOL
HOLDER
TABLE
BASE
STEP 4.
CARRIAGE
LINK
CRANK PIN
COLUMN
FLYWHEEL
MOTOR
ROCKER ARM

Fig. 10D

chalkwork 10D

Constructing the Progressive Diagram. Example: The Shaping Machine. Work from the basic idea of a source of power driving a reciprocating tool.

1 Lightly sketch a square for the column. Develop the idea of the drive by drawing in the motor, the gearing, the flywheel and the crank pin. Discuss the column, the carriage and the bed extension and draw in, adding all labels. Fig. 10D, step 1.

2 Develop the details of connecting the carriage with the flywheel and so add the rocker arm and link, Fig. 10D, step 2.

3 Progress to the tool head with its graduated disc, slide and spindle, clapper box, toolholder and tool, Fig. 10D, step 3.

4 Add the table and the base and complete the labelling, Fig. 10D, step 4.

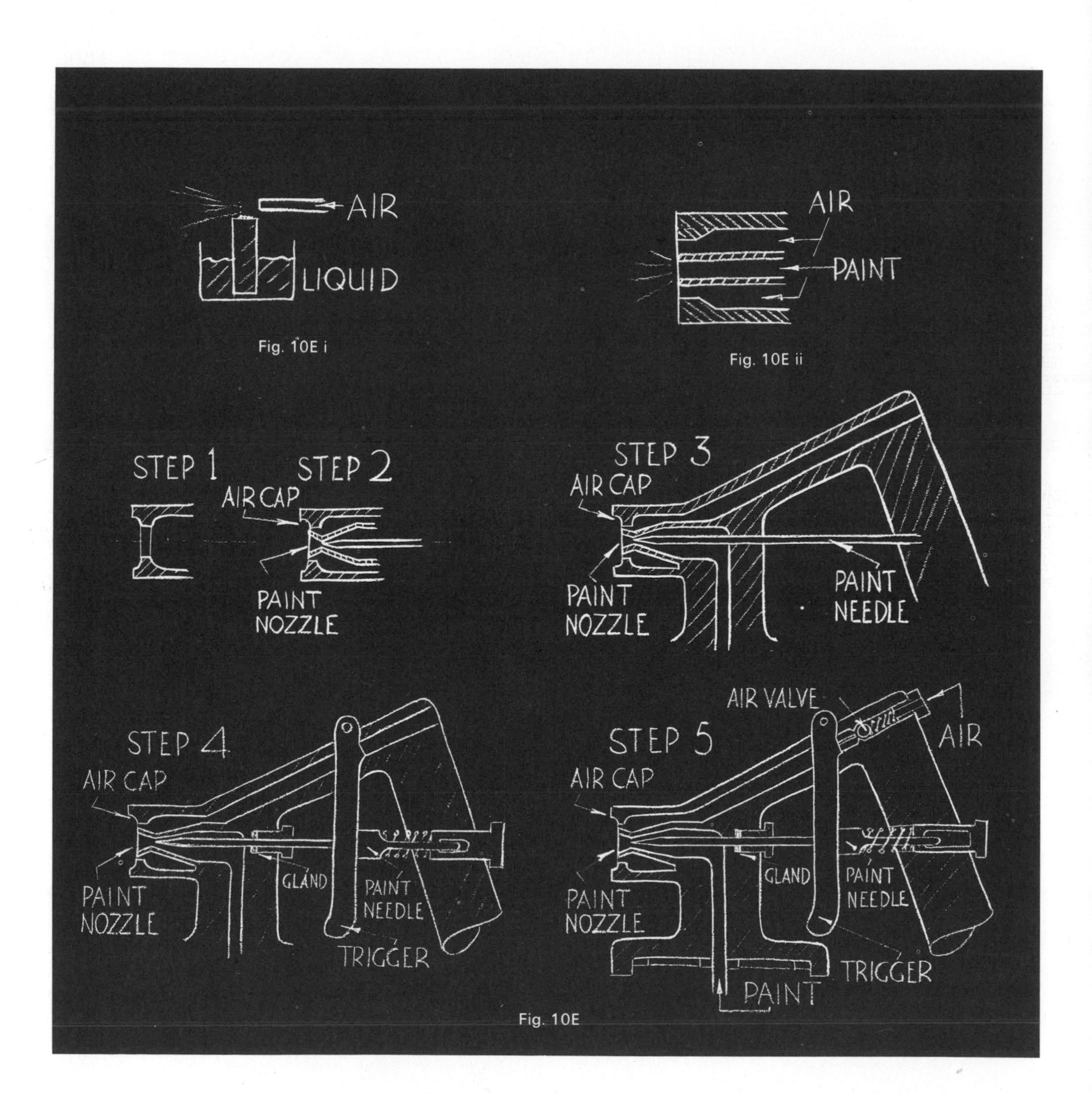
AIR
LIQUID
Fig. 10E i
AIR
PAINT
Fig. 10E ii
STEP 1
STEP 2
AIR CAP
PAINT
NOZZLE
STEP 3
AIR CAP
PAINT
NOZZLE
PAINT
NEEDLE
STEP 4
AIR CAP
PAINT
NOZZLE
GLAND
PAINT
NEEDLE
TRIGGER
AIR VALVE
STEP 5
AIR
AIR CAP
PAINT
NOZZLE
GLAND
PAINT
NEEDLE
TRIGGER
PAINT
Fig. 10E

chalkwork 10E

Making the progressive diagram. Example: The Spray Gun. Two preliminary diagrams Figs. 10E i and 10E ii are needed in this example for establishing the principle of the siphon-type gun. The main diagram grows from Fig. 10E ii through accommodating the three requirements of controlling the shape of the air stream, controlling the supply of the air stream and controlling the supply of paint.

1 Lightly draw in a rectangle for the air cap. Explain the shape of the inside and the shape of the lugs, then draw in. Add the centre line for future use, Fig. 10E, step 1.

2 Explain the shaping of the paint nozzle as a modification of a tube and add to the drawing, Fig. 10E, step 2.

3 Continue the paint nozzle to the feed tube, turning it downwards. Extend the paint needle and draw in the body shape, adding the labels. Fig. 10E, step 3.

4 Explain the trigger, the paint control mechanism and the gland, adding in stages with labels, Fig. 10E, step 4.

5 Continue to the air control valve and the trigger connecting mechanism, adding the appropriate labels. Extend the neck of the paint cup fixing ring to complete this diagram. Fig. 10E, step 5.

A drawing of this complexity, done free hand, needs a level of skill which comes from experience and practice. Do not expect to acquire this level too soon, but keep it in mind as your target of attainment.

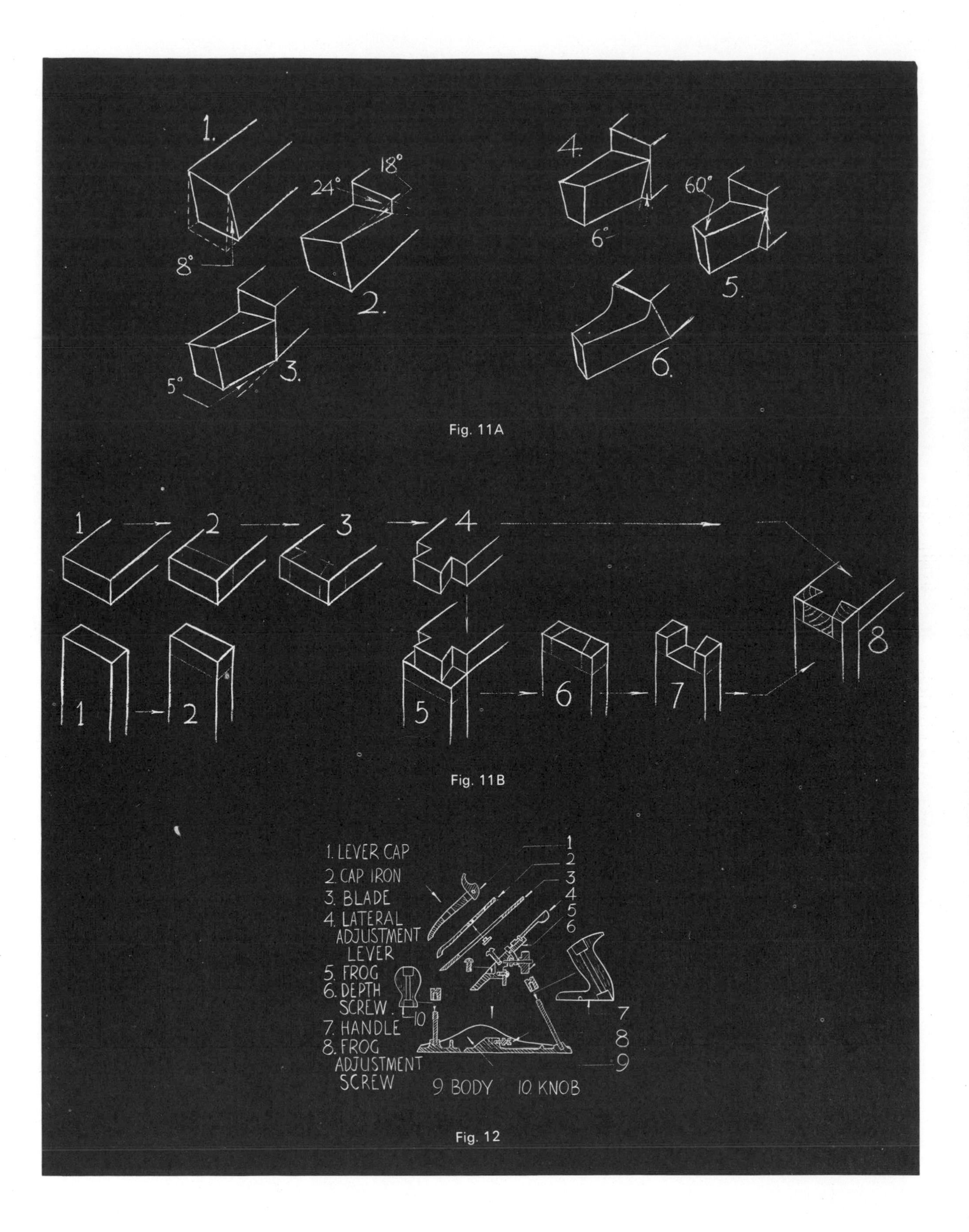

Fig. 11A

Fig. 11B

Fig. 12

chalkwork 11

THE STRIP DIAGRAM

1 In the previous examples of the progressive diagram the early stages are incorporated into the following stages, i.e. one diagram is achieved at the end of the teaching. Some subjects demand a series of diagrams, each one developing from or connected with the previous one, yet each a distinct feature in itself. The shaping of a lathe tool in Fig. 11A is an example. The critical teaching factor is not the embodiment of all the data in step 6 but how step 6 is achieved. This demands separate recordings of each stage. (The angles are shown sharp for clarity until step 6 is reached.)

2 The technique of guide lines with addition in small stages is as before. Where there is repetition of a shape, it can be advantageous to make a stout paper cut-out template to be used for the light layout in each stage. If the diagrams are drawn as the lesson is developed, then the diagram can be termed a Progressive Strip Diagram. If the illustration is complete before the teaching starts then it can be termed a Prepared Strip Diagram.

3 Figure 11B is a strip diagram for the making of a dovetail joint. This kind of progression in stages is very useful for the job analysis (work procedure) in workshop teaching. The spacing-out of the diagram can be such as to emphasise the progression in the content.

chalkwork 12

THE EXPLODED DIAGRAM

Information about covered detail usually is given by using sectional views, but often the complexity of the parts when fitted together makes clarity of seeing difficult. This difficulty can be overcome by drawing apart or exploding the component parts. For optimum effect keep a relationship between the exploded placing and the original position, thus obtaining a separation for clarity and a sense of connection for understanding. Figure 12 shows an exploded section of a steel smoothing-plane.

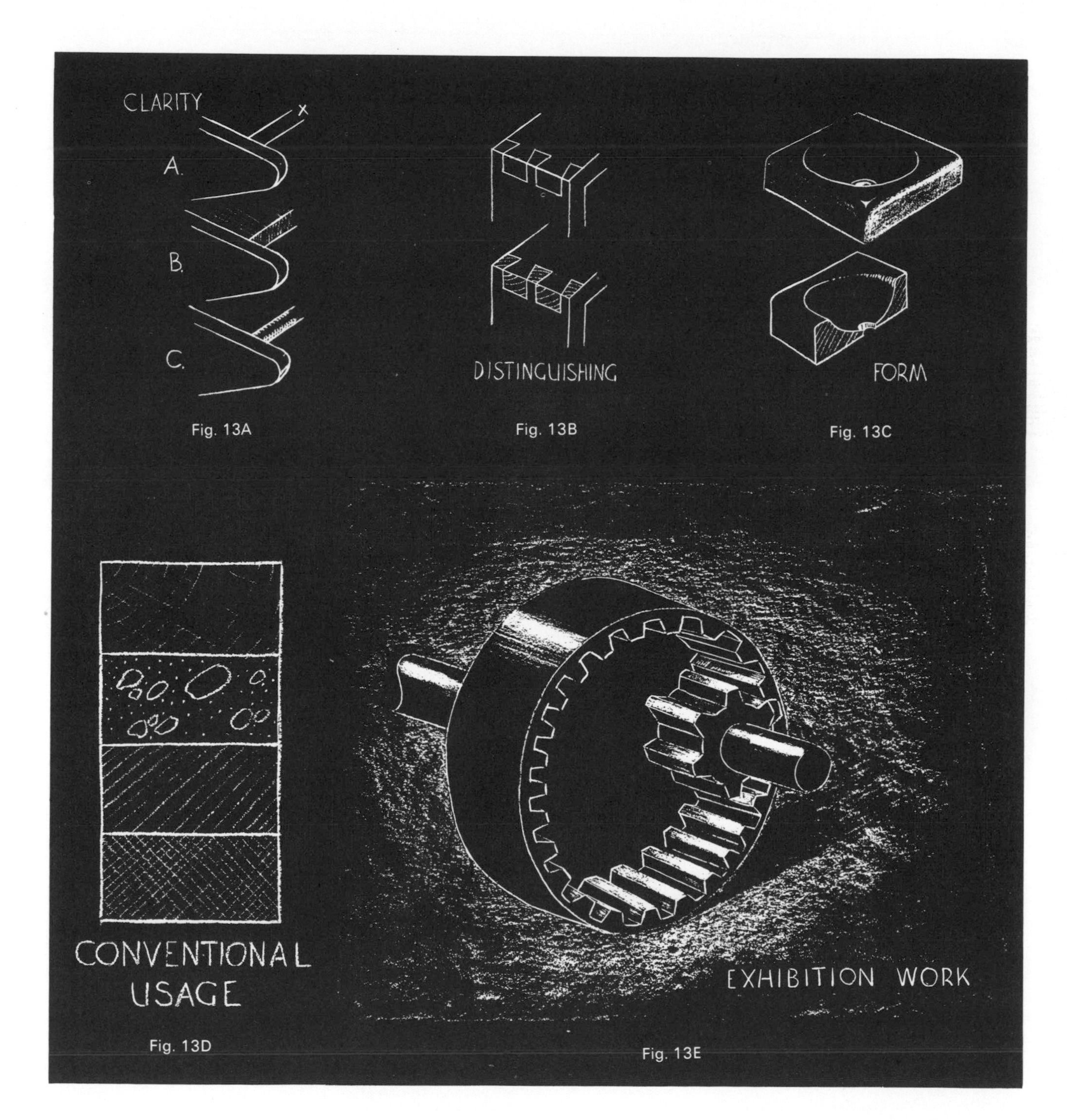

Fig. 13A

Fig. 13B

Fig. 13C

Fig. 13D

Fig. 13E

chalkwork 13

SHADING AND COLOURING

1 When shading is used it must serve some purpose to justify the extra time involved, such as:

a) To clarify the information in the drawing. In Fig. 13A the information given by the lines *x* is unclear. It could be interpreted as either B or C. Shading clarifies this information.

b) To distinguish one part from another, Fig. 13B.

c) To achieve moulded forms, Fig. 13C.

d) To observe some conventional practice which carries meaning, Fig. 13D.

e) To attract in exhibition work, Fig. 13E.

The most common method of shading is cross hatching, and by placing the strokes close together opaqueness can be achieved. Double cross hatching will give greater intensity. This method is slow. Quick coverage may be achieved by using the chalk flatwise and obtaining intensity by either greater pressure or a second coat.

2 Colour work also must be used purposefully, to emphasise, to differentiate, to obey convention or to provide attraction. One part of a diagram may be picked out from another by change of colour; attention may be drawn to an important fact in writing, by using coloured chalk; or information may be given by observing a certain colour convention, e.g. in hydraulics, red will indicate fluid under pressure. The emphasis gained from the use of colour rests in its rarity of usage.

Fig. 14A

Fig. 14B

Fig. 14C

chalkwork 14

BLACKBOARD INSTRUMENT WORK

1 Chalkwork drawing instruments are used when there is need for one or more of the following:

a) Accurate proportions.
b) Exact dimension.
c) Precise construction.
d) Specific techniques of draughtsmanship.
e) High quality execution when intricacy of detail is present.

2 The standard of the teacher's chalkwork in the Drawing Period can be such as to challenge and inspire the student in his standard of pencil work.

3 a) Make sure that the instruments and the left-hand edge of the chalk-board are in good condition.

b) Have plenty of sharpened chalk. See Chalkwork 6, section 7. If you have access to a double-ended grinder this need is easily fulfilled. There is a type of chalk in large rectangular sticks which is excellent for the Drawing Lesson.

c) Be capable of drawing the various types of lines. The early exercises for lines of graded intensity, for broken lines, for dimension lines, etc., should be practised, using firstly the straight edge, and then the board compasses. Figures 14A and 14B.

d) The drawing of vertical lines in accordance with drawing board practice presents difficulty. One way is to make a tall set square which can slide along a true slip of wood screwed to the lower edge of the chalk-board.

e) The construction in a drawing can confuse the finished result. Keep the construction lines light, and make a pre-practice for best positioning.

f) The teacher is always an example to the class. Set the standard in draughtsmanship and drawing practice.

4 For isometric work it is useful to have part of the board scored with an isometric grid, Fig. 14C. To do this, set out the grid in pencil, then cut the surface of the board with a knife. The chalk dust will collect in the cut marks and keep them well defined.

5 Plywood templates of geometrical figures, e.g. the ellipse, can be very useful. See Figs. 15G and 15H.

6 Figures 14D and 14E show samples of blackboard instrument work from the classroom and workshop respectively.

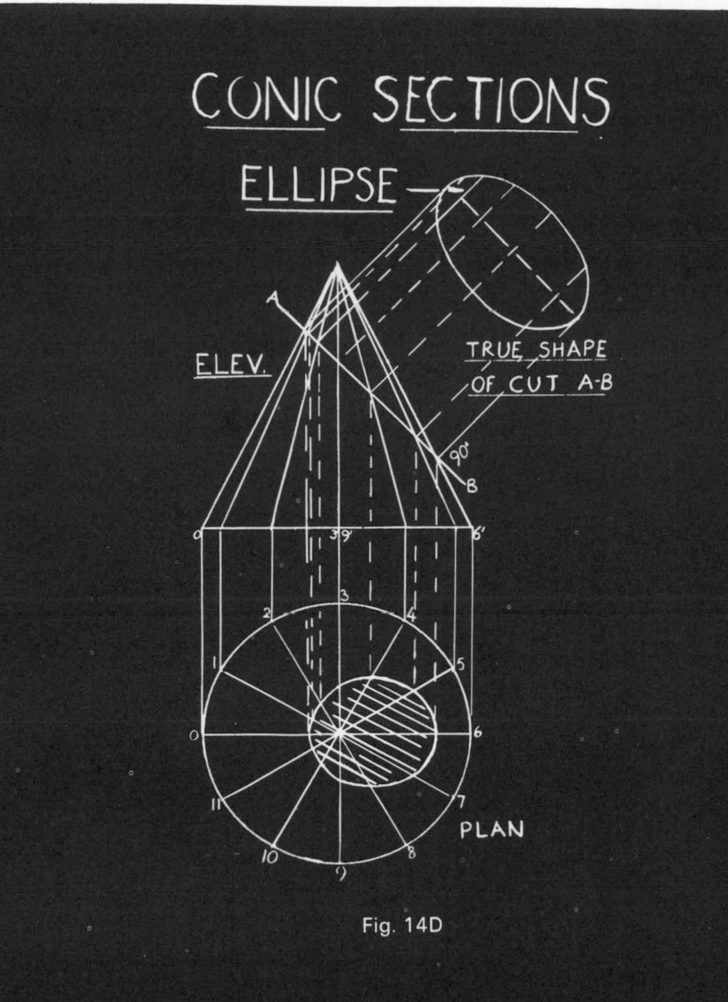

Fig. 14D

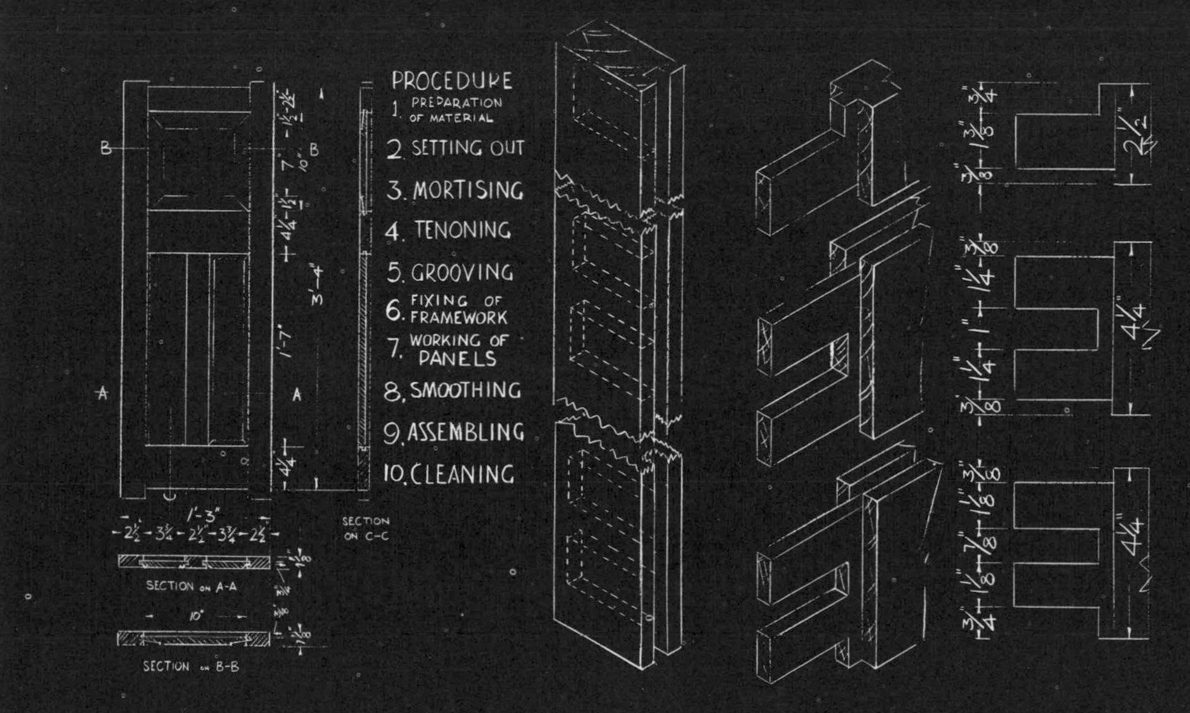

Fig. 14E

prepared work and charts 1

GENERAL

1 The teacher finds that he uses two types of prepared illustrations, viz.

a) Personal, i.e. made by the teacher.

b) Commercial, i.e. made by some outside firm or body.

Each type has its place in teaching, and each type should be used to the most effective end.

The personal illustration is highly selective and always available. The commercial one is usually finely produced, very complete and very detailed. Be careful in your selection. Over-complicated diagrams, however attractive, are not very helpful in teaching.

2 Prepared diagrams are used by the teacher:

a) When the complexity of the content is too great to permit progressive building concurrent with the teaching.

b) When the actual making of the diagram has no significance to the understanding of content being taught.

c) For pre-lesson interest or post-lesson discussion.

3 When a prepared diagram is used because of complexity of content, it is sound practice to simplify the content to the essential facts and principles through a progressive diagram, and then to follow on with the prepared chart. This is one of the effective ways of using a commercial chart.

If several charts are to be used it is essential to have them under control for easy manipulation during the lesson. Working out how this is to be done is part of lesson preparation.

4 There is a hybrid form of chart which is part commercial and part personal. Illustrations are collected from periodicals, papers, etc., and then the teacher compiles a chart for his specific purpose by mounting the selected cuttings on a large sheet and adding his own labels and notes. The basic material is commercial, the compilation is personal.

5 It is possible to use prepared diagrams in a progressive manner by having a series of charts each developed one stage more in the work than the previous one. As the exposition proceeds, so the more developed diagrams are brought out, until the final diagram is the completed subject matter. The diagrams of the spray gun in Chalkwork 10E, page 30, could be used in this manner.

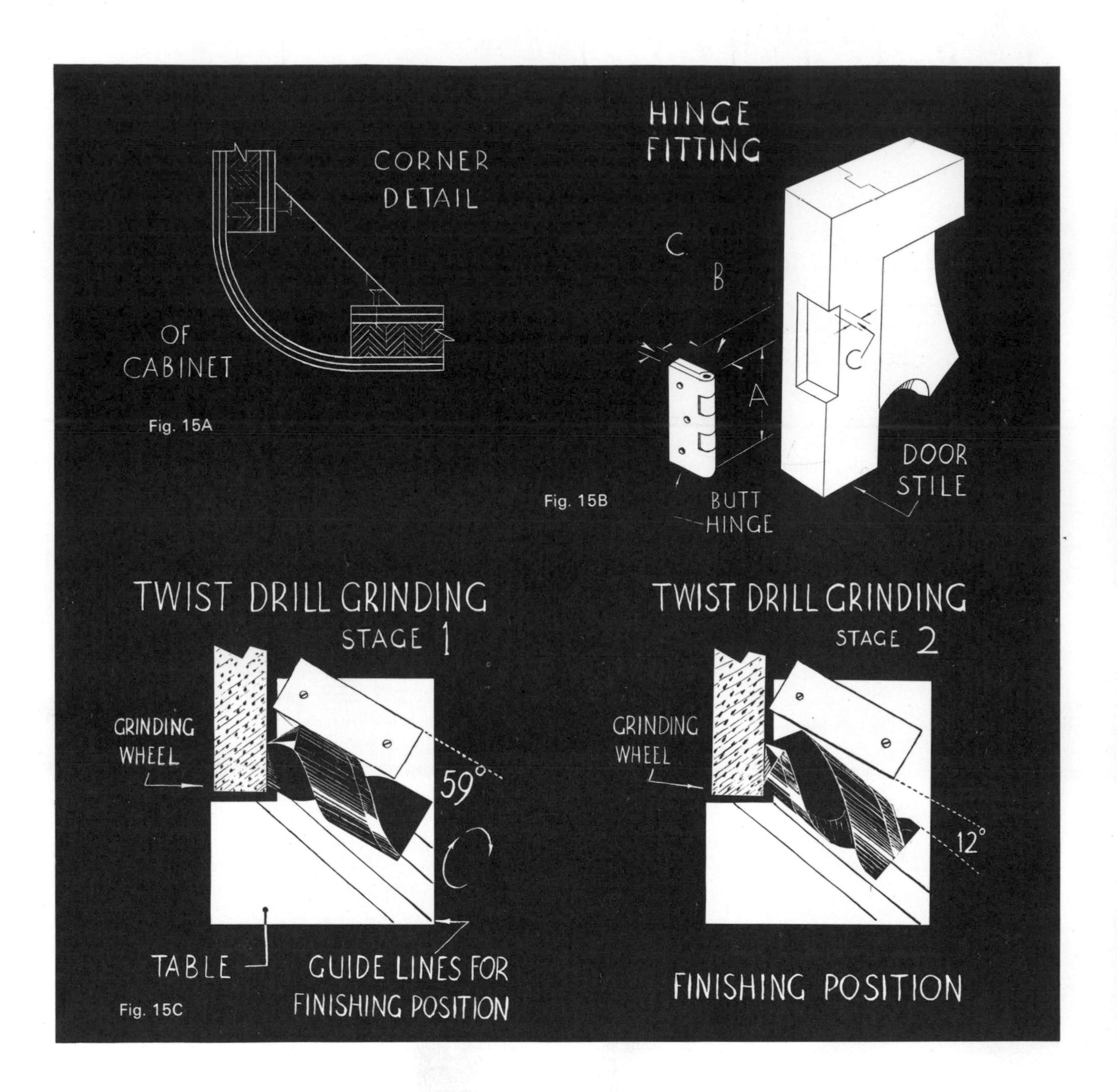

Fig. 15A

Fig. 15B

Fig. 15C

e) Set out the lettering on pieces of scrap paper, adjusting the size and spacing by trial and error. Then complete the lettering on the chart in the light of the knowledge gained from the scrap paper lettering. This method will avoid spoiling the chart by misplaced and cramped lettering.

f) Add the connecting arrows.
Note i. It is often convenient to work up the entire shape of the main parts of a diagram on a trial piece of paper and then to cut out the shapes and use them as templates for the guide image on the chart.
ii. The chart must be large enough to do its job efficiently.

prepared work and charts 2

CHART MAKING

1 The chart must possess two qualities to satisfy the teacher:

a) It must be effective, i.e. clear, powerful and attractive.

b) It must not consume too much time in being produced.

2 The media for chart making are:

a) **Chalk and Pastel** (a finer type of chalk).

These are very intense media, speedy in use and familiar. The disadvantages are the lack of permanency through smudging, the difficulty of dealing with fine detail and the picking up of chalk dust on parts of the chart where it is not wanted.

b) **Wax Crayon** (coloured pencil).

This may be obtained in a range of colours in either stick or pencil form. It is easy to use either free-hand or with instruments; it is permanent and fairly intense; it is clean and it will accommodate a high degree of fineness and accuracy. Figure 15A shows a white crayon drawing on black paper. Try this media using blue or black crayon on white paper.

c) **Poster Paints and Coloured Inks.**

These media may be used with either drawing instruments for mechanical drawing or brush for free-hand work. They are intense, permanent and accommodating for intricate work, but they are time consuming and difficult in usage. For diagrams needing areas of contrast they are very effective. Figure 15B shows an application of white ink and black ink on black paper.

d) **Contrasting Paper.**

Contrasting masses in a chart give clarity and attraction. These areas of contrast can be made in cut-out shapes of different coloured papers which are stuck on to the background. The detail of the content can then be worked on top. Figure 15C shows an example in white paper on a black ground with white and black ink used for detailing.

3 **Procedure.**

a) Make preliminary small sketches of the analysis of the content, remembering that it is better to make two charts each with a single piece of information than one chart with two pieces of information.

b) Make a trial layout for location. Scrap paper cut to the approximate size and shape can be useful for trial and error tests. Do not overfill the chart, but use all the space to obtain the requisite size.

c) Place in the guide lines or the guide image. Ordinary pencil is useful here.

d) Complete in the chosen medium.

continued opposite

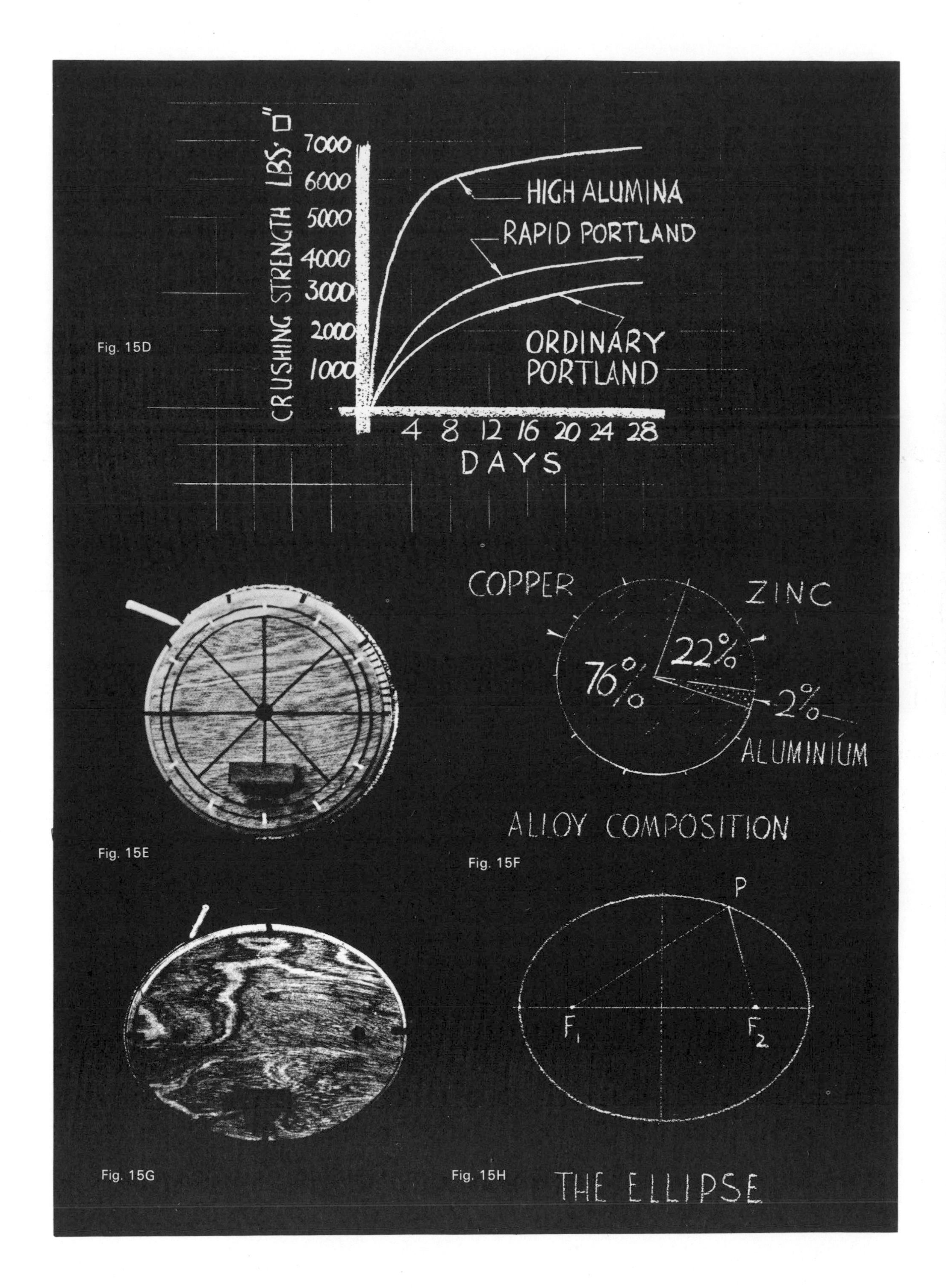

Fig. 15D

Fig. 15E

Fig. 15F

Fig. 15G

Fig. 15H

prepared work and charts 3

SOME PROBLEMS

1 **Measurement.**

When correctness of dimension is needed to make the diagram effective there is a slowing down of the rate of production. This can be minimised by using squared paper of large size for charts, or by having part of the blackboard scored with a squared grid. See Chalkwork 14, section 4. Figure 15D shows a scored board used for making a graph on the setting of cements. For the pie diagram, i.e. a circle subdivided into proportional parts, a graduated plywood disc is useful. The marked divisions should be tenths, twelfths and eighths, with one tenth division subdivided for the hundredth when using percentages. Figure 15E shows a disc and Fig. 15F its application.

---

2 **Standard Shapes.**

The plywood template is also very useful in drawing standard shapes, particularly if the shape is difficult. Figure 15G shows an ellipse template and Fig. 15H its application.

For setting out an ellipse in making a template, the string method is very convenient. An ellipse is a plane figure traced by a point which moves so that the sum of its distances from two fixed points, called foci, is constant.

Knock into a piece of plywood two nails (the foci) separated by a distance of about $\frac{2}{3}$ of the maximum dimension of the ellipse desired. Take a piece of string about $1\frac{1}{2}$ times the distance between the nails, and tie the ends, one to each nail. The string will be slack. With a piece of chalk (or pencil) tighten the string to form a triangle between the chalk and the two nails. Now trace out a line keeping the string taut. The figure so drawn will be an ellipse because the sum of the distances of the chalk from the two nails remained the same, viz., the length of the string. For more detail on drawing an ellipse, refer to a textbook on Geometrical Drawing.

---

3 **Mass.**

When mass effect is required the previously mentioned methods of cut paper or flat chalk may be used. If the areas are to be differentiated, different forms of shading may be used and a "key" or "legend" given for the meaning.

Figure 15 I shows a quarter-section of a tree trunk. The various parts of the wood growth can be well illustrated by using the key method of shading.

---

4 **Fixing Chalkwork.**

The sheet may be sprayed with a mouth spray and "fixative" obtained from suppliers of school materials. If access is available to a spray plant and materials, the sheet may be sprayed with a thin solution of furniture lacquer, of the proportions: one part lacquer to three parts thinners. For occasions of emergency, ladies' hair spray will be found effective.

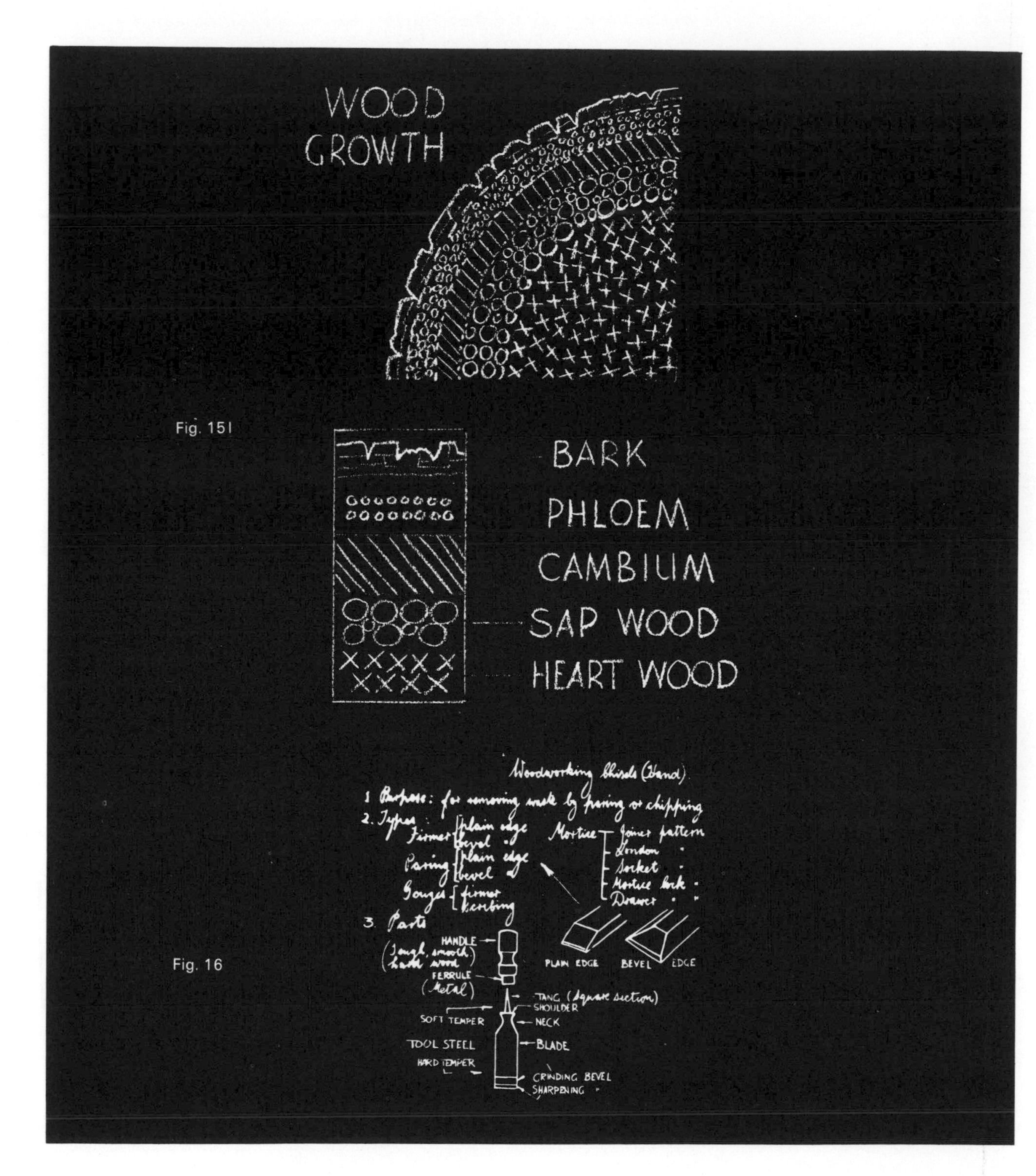

Fig. 15I

Fig. 16

review and preview

The aims of the previous chapters were:

a) To help in producing an effective teaching illustration.
b) To help in recording lesson content.
c) To help in obtaining full teaching impact from the illustration.

Figure 16 shows a part blackboard summary, of a lengthy topic, on a board of limited area. At this stage of recording, all step 3 would be cleaned off and the specialised information of the first type of chisel from step 2, viz., the firmer chisel, would be added. This process of clearing and adding would be repeated until the whole topic is recorded.

This summary is of the mixed note and diagram kind, the diagrams being of two distinct types. The one of the parts of a chisel is a flat diagram, showing the chisel handle drawn away (exploded) from the blade for clarity of detail. The other diagram, showing the plain edge and bevel edge, chisel forms, is a three-dimensional representation, which is sometimes called a pictorial drawing or a perspective drawing. This type of teaching illustration is the subject of the following chapters, which show how to make a perspective drawing of a technical object by being able to draw the geometrical solids which compose the object.

Perspective illustration can play a very effective part in teaching because of its immediate and easy appeal. The teacher should try to develop a sense of pictorial visualisation so that he can select the choice of view which gives the maximum information with the greatest clarity.

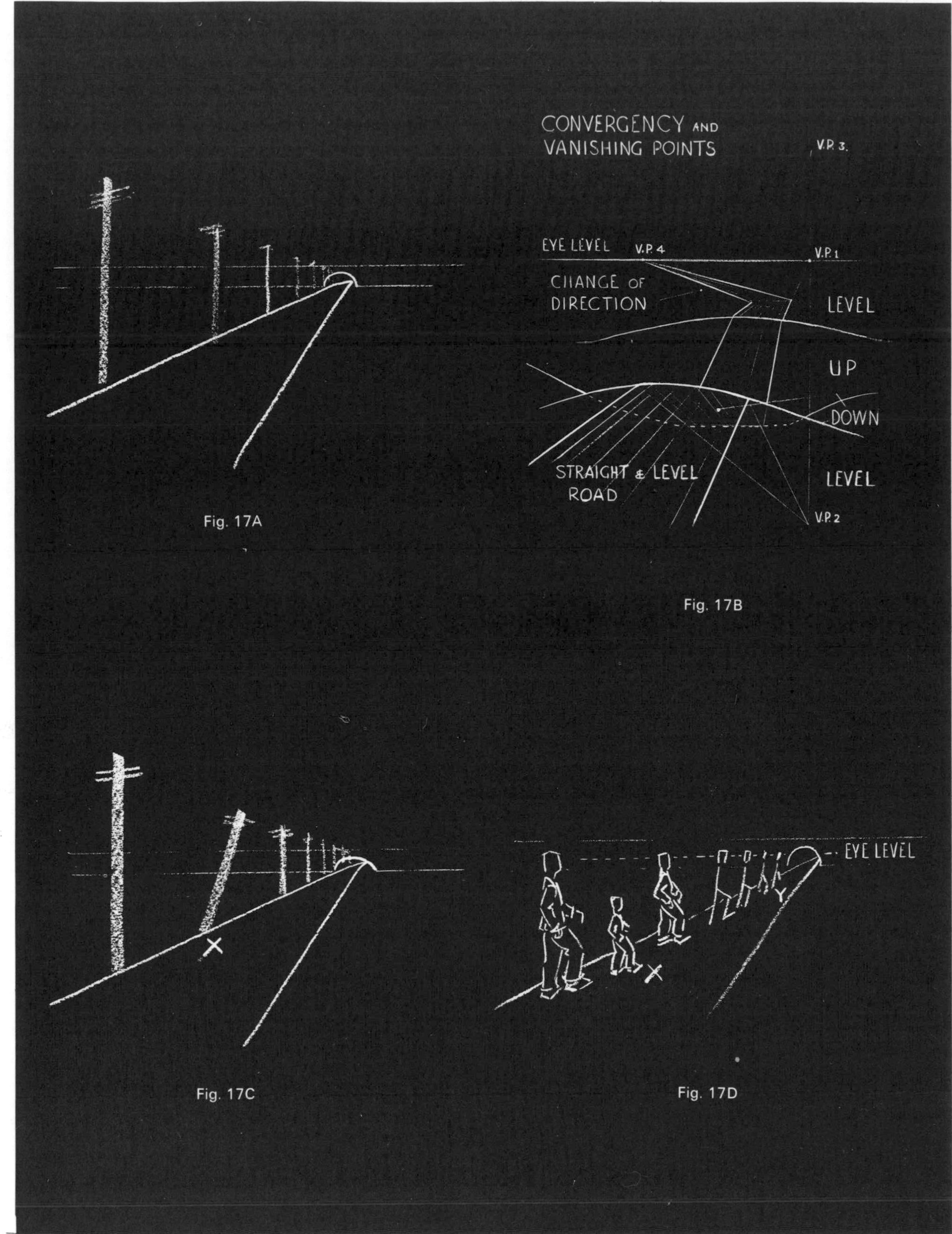

Fig. 17A

Fig. 17B

Fig. 17C

Fig. 17D

free-hand perspective drawing 1

THE BASIC RULES

The basic rules of perspective drawing are known through common observation.

1 Look at Fig. 17A. The parallel lines which recede, i.e. go away into the distance, appear to converge. The lines forming the road, and the line limiting the poles, form a set of parallel lines which converge on the drawing to a common point. Such a point is called a vanishing point. Lines which do not recede do not have convergency. The lines forming the railway embankment are without convergency and the vertical lines forming the poles are also without convergency.

2 Look at Fig. 17B. This is a diagram of a road going away into the distance. The road starts level, note the vanishing point VP1; then it goes down hill, note VP2; then it goes uphill, note VP3; then it goes level again and in the first direction, before it changes direction to VP4. Groups of horizontal parallel lines find their vanishing points on the eye-level. Groups of tilted parallel lines have their vanishing points above or below the eye-level. This information is interesting, but not too important in the making of a classroom perspective diagram.

3 Vertical lines are drawn vertical. In Fig. 17C, it is obvious that pole *x* is falling over. If one wishes it to look vertical, it must be drawn vertical.

4 Perspective sizes are relative. In Fig. 17D the person *X* is obviously small, yet in actual dimension it is larger than person *Y*. Sizes are relative to positioning in the illustration.

The procedure for making a perspective illustration is as follows:

1 The vertical lines of the object are drawn vertical in the illustration.

2 The horizontal lines of the object are drawn with a slope in the illustration, those below the eye-level sloping upwards, and those above the eye-level sloping downwards, as they go away from the nearest corner of the object. This corner may be real or imaginary.

3 The groups of parallel, horizontal lines of the object are drawn with a convergency in the illustration, and they converge as they go away from the nearest corner.

4 The non-horizontal lines of the object are drawn by estimation, using vertical and horizontal lines to help.

5 Perspective proportions are estimated.

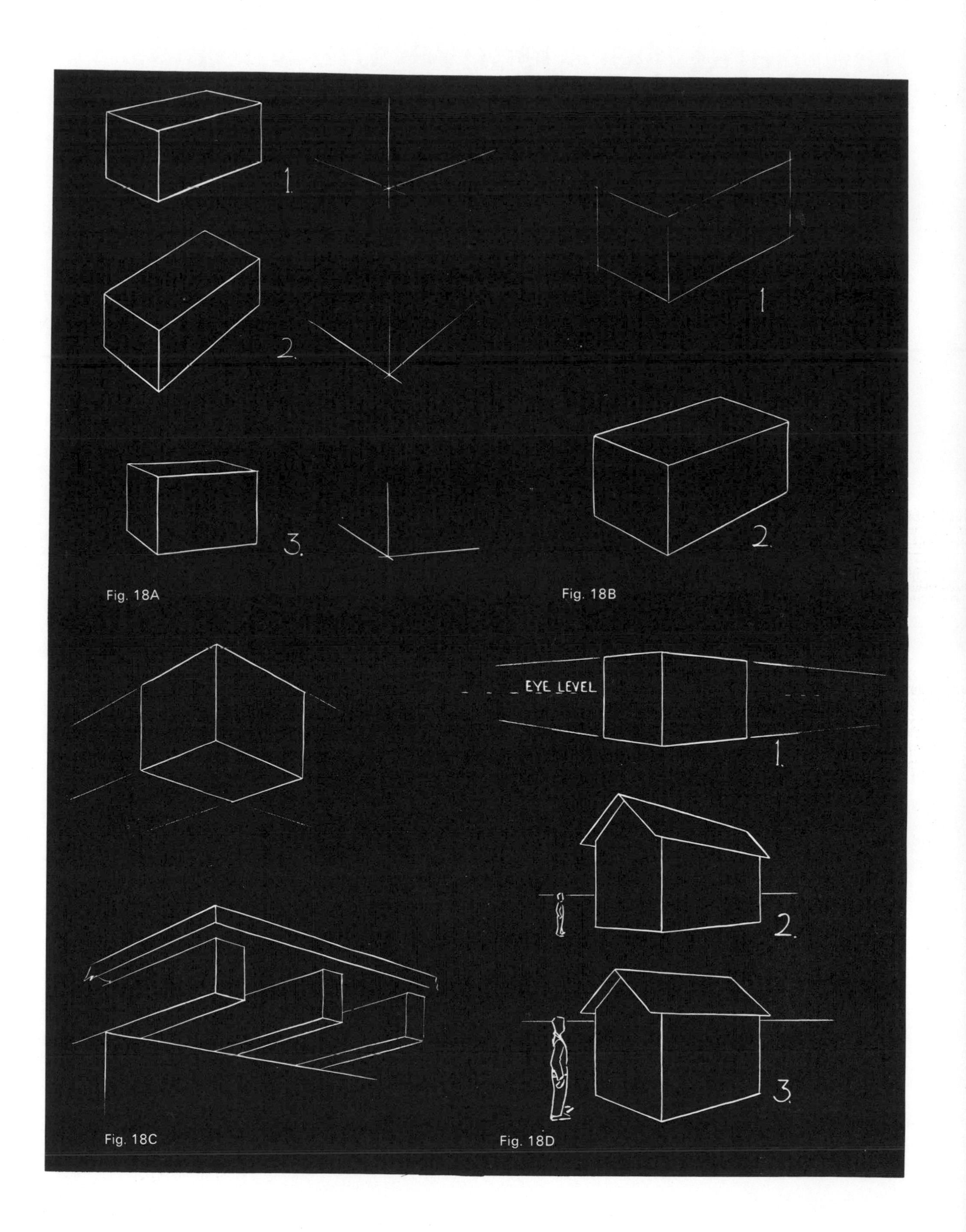

Fig. 18A

Fig. 18B

Fig. 18C

Fig. 18D

free-hand perspective drawing 2

THE HORIZONTAL BOX

A Position below the Eye-level.

1 Start with the nearest corner guide line, then draw the two bottom edges giving a slope of about 30°, Fig. 18A 1. This slope may be increased to give a drawing showing more of the top, Fig. 18A 2, or decreased for less of the top. The slope angles may be varied individually to show more of one side, and less of the other, Fig. 18A 3. Remember, the less shown of a side the greater the slope angle for a given proportion.

2 Cut off the desired proportions by vertical lines, Fig. 18B 1.

3 Complete the setting out with converging lines, estimating the convergency for the correctness of impression.

4 Line in with a clear, strong line, Fig. 18B 2.

B Position above the Eye-level.
Repeat the above-mentioned steps. The convergency is downwards as the lines move away from the nearest corner, Fig. 18C.
This position shows the underside of the box.

C Position on the Eye-level.
In this position neither top nor bottom is visible.

1 Start with the nearest corner. Give an upward slope to the base lines, and a downward slope to the top lines.

2 Cut off the proportions and line in, Fig. 18D 1.
The slopes chosen set the position of the eye-level for the drawing. This is the line joining the meeting points of the pairs of top and bottom edges produced. It should be horizontal. The position of the eye-level is important in creating the impression of size. Figures 18D 2 and 3 show similar shapes at different eye-level positions, to create firstly the impression of a large building and secondly a small building.

Fig. 18E

Fig. 18F

Fig. 18G

Fig. 18H

Fig. 18I

exercises for the horizontal box

1. Draw three simple boxes below the eye-level, varying the positions to show equal top and sides, emphasis on the top, and emphasis on one side.
2. Try some above eye-level examples.
3. Try some on the eye-level examples. If you choose a building, e.g. a petrol station, keep to simple box shapes.
4. Try Fig. 18E for estimating perspective sizes.
5. Try Fig. 18F, a bridle joint, for connecting perspective levels. (This is an example of an exploded view.)
6. Try Fig. 18G, a set of steps, for a wide range of slope angles. Note the step on the eye-level.
7. Try Fig. 18H, a triangular frame, for non-horizontal parallels. The nearer the parallels to vertical, the less the convergency.
8. Figure 18 I shows a tilted box. Note the convergency of the groups of parallel lines as they go away from the nearest corner. Inclination is best shown in classroom illustrations, by letting it contrast with some obvious vertical or horizontal feature in the drawing.

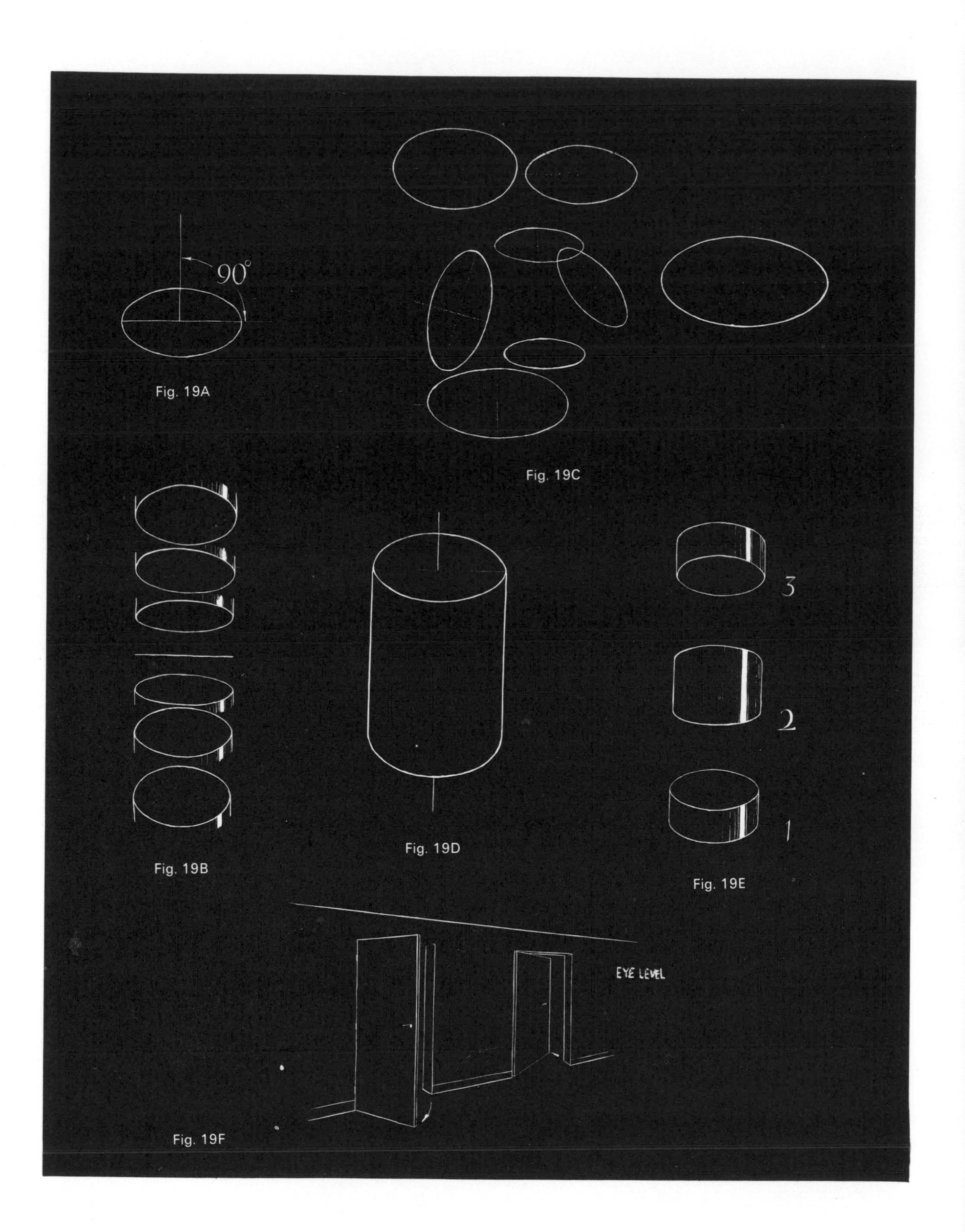

Fig. 19A

Fig. 19C

Fig. 19B

Fig. 19D

Fig. 19E

Fig. 19F

free-hand perspective drawing 3

THE VERTICAL CYLINDER

1 The circular end of the cylinder as it is seen becomes an ellipse, with its major axis at right-angles to the axis of the cylinder, Fig. 19A. This is the most important rule for drawing cylinders, and it applies to the cylinder in any position.

2 Figure 19B shows how the proportions of the ellipse vary in the various positions relative to the eye-level.

3 To shape an ellipse in free-hand drawing, mould the shape in continuous light strokes, then line in boldly the chosen shape, Fig. 19C.

4 To draw a vertical cylinder, make a light vertical stroke for the axis, then lightly draw in an ellipse of the chosen proportions according to the view. Draw the two vertical lines for the sides, and lightly sketch in the lower ellipse. Line in boldly; firstly the full ellipse, then the sides and finally the half ellipse, making sure that the sides join smoothly into the ellipses, Fig. 19D.

5 The cylinder on the eye-level lacks impact, Fig. 19E 2, but it has a useful application in craftwork free sketching for hinged doors. Figure 19F shows two doors swung in opposite directions.

6 The cylinder above the eye-level is drawn in the same manner, viz. the vertical axis, the full ellipse, the sides, the half ellipse, and the lining in Fig. 19E 3.

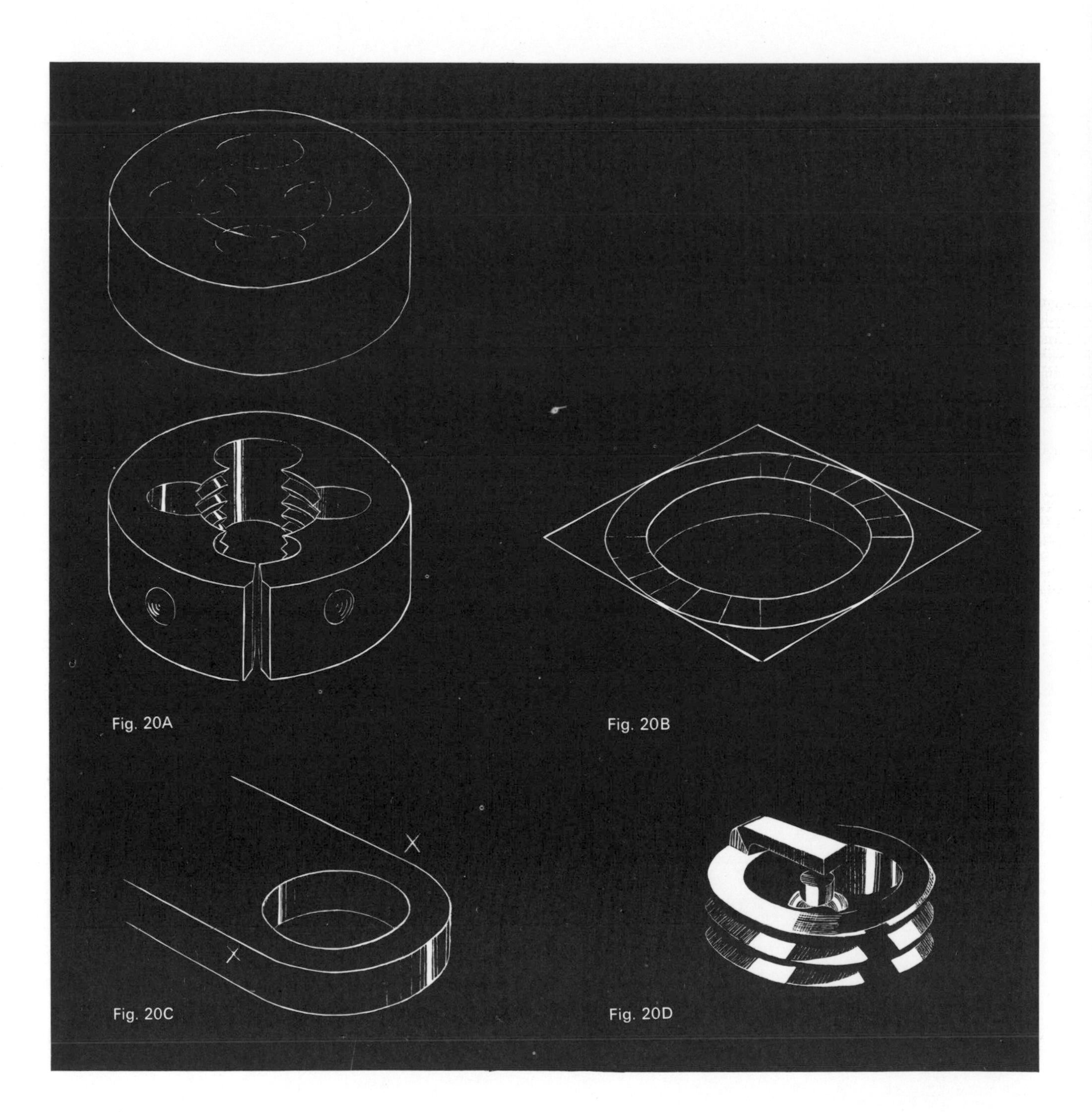

Fig. 20A

Fig. 20B

Fig. 20C

Fig. 20D

exercises for the vertical cylinder

1. Practise samples of various ellipses with horizontal major axes, varying the sizes, i.e. varying both major and minor axes, and then varying the shapes for perspective positioning relative to the eye-level, i.e. keeping the major axis constant and changing the minor axis.

2. Practise below and above eye-level examples of ellipses adding the side strokes as in Fig. 19B.

3. Draw an average cylinder for teaching purposes, Fig. 19D.

4. Try Fig. 20A. This drawing of an engineer's die emphasises the horizontal quality of the ellipses, and it also gives good practice in perspective spacing out.

5. Try Fig. 20B. This drawing of a paved circular pond shows firstly the value of using a perspective square as a guide for a perspective circle, and secondly the value of perspective diameters in setting out detail.

6. Figure 20C shows a metal strip with a semi-circular end. The perspective diameter *X–X* is used to give perspective proportions for the semicircle.

7. Figure 20D is a drawing of the points of a sparking plug. Ellipses are used in setting out the shapes for mass effect, a treatment which is best restricted to exhibition work.

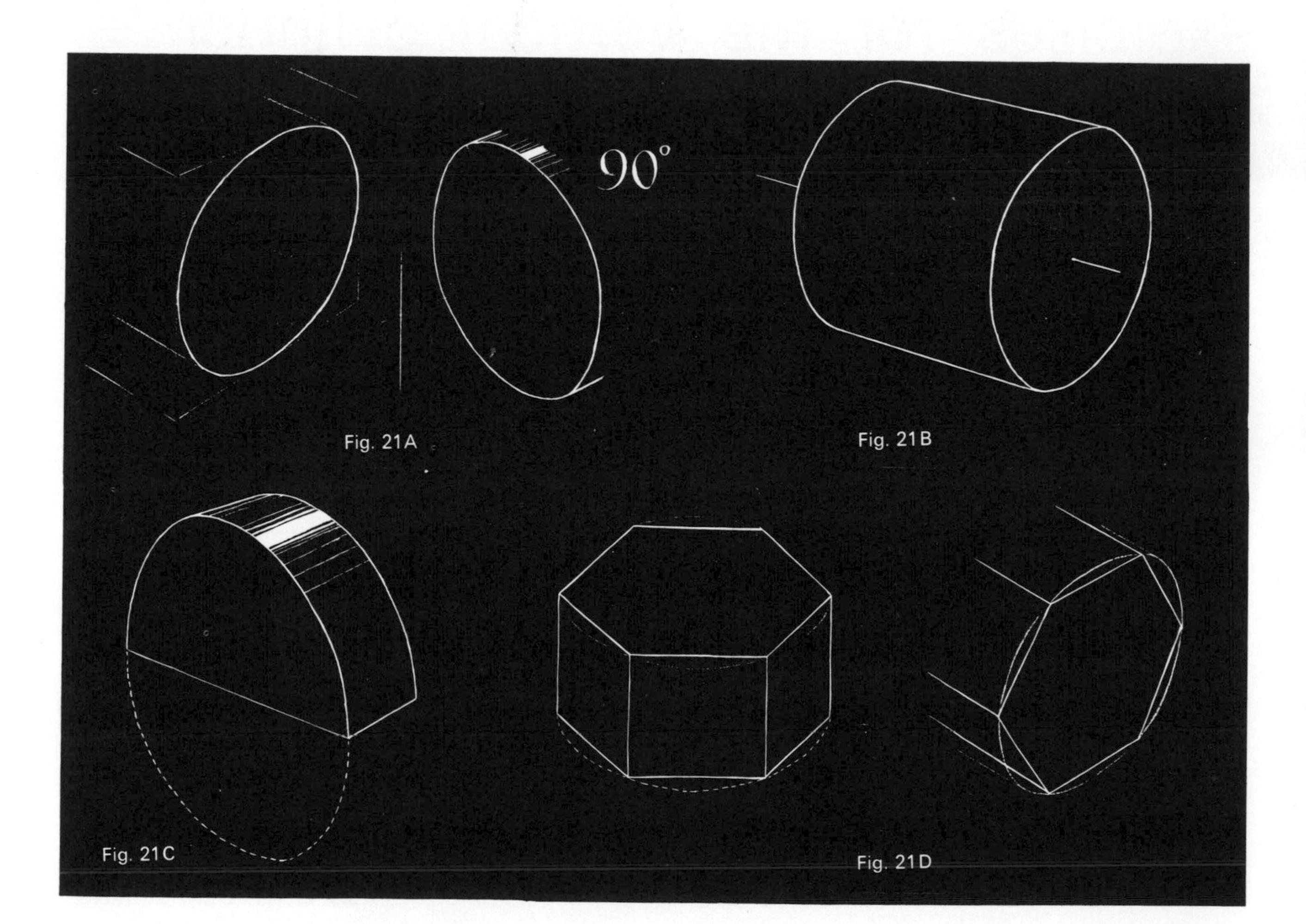

Fig. 21A

Fig. 21B

Fig. 21C

Fig. 21D

free-hand perspective drawing 4

THE HORIZONTAL CYLINDER

1 The previous rules apply for drawing the cylinder in this position, viz., that parallel horizontal lines have convergency with recession, and that the major axis of the ellipse is at right-angles to the axis of the cylinder, Fig. 21A.

2 To draw a horizontal cylinder proceed as follows: draw a light line for the perspective axis of the cylinder, then sketch in lightly the nearer ellipse with its major axis at right-angles to this line. Light perspective horizontal lines are then drawn, observing the convergency quality, and then the far ellipse is set into the estimated shape. The cylinder is then lined in boldly, Fig. 21B.

3 A semi-cylinder is cut off by a perspective diameter, Fig. 21C.

4 A cylinder is often used for setting out other right prisms. Figure 21D shows an example of the hexagonal prism.

5 Cylinders on the eye-level, and above the eye-level have limited application to classroom illustration, but they may be drawn for practice following the same procedure as set out above. Figure 22A shows two semi-circular arches constructed from cylinders above eye-level.

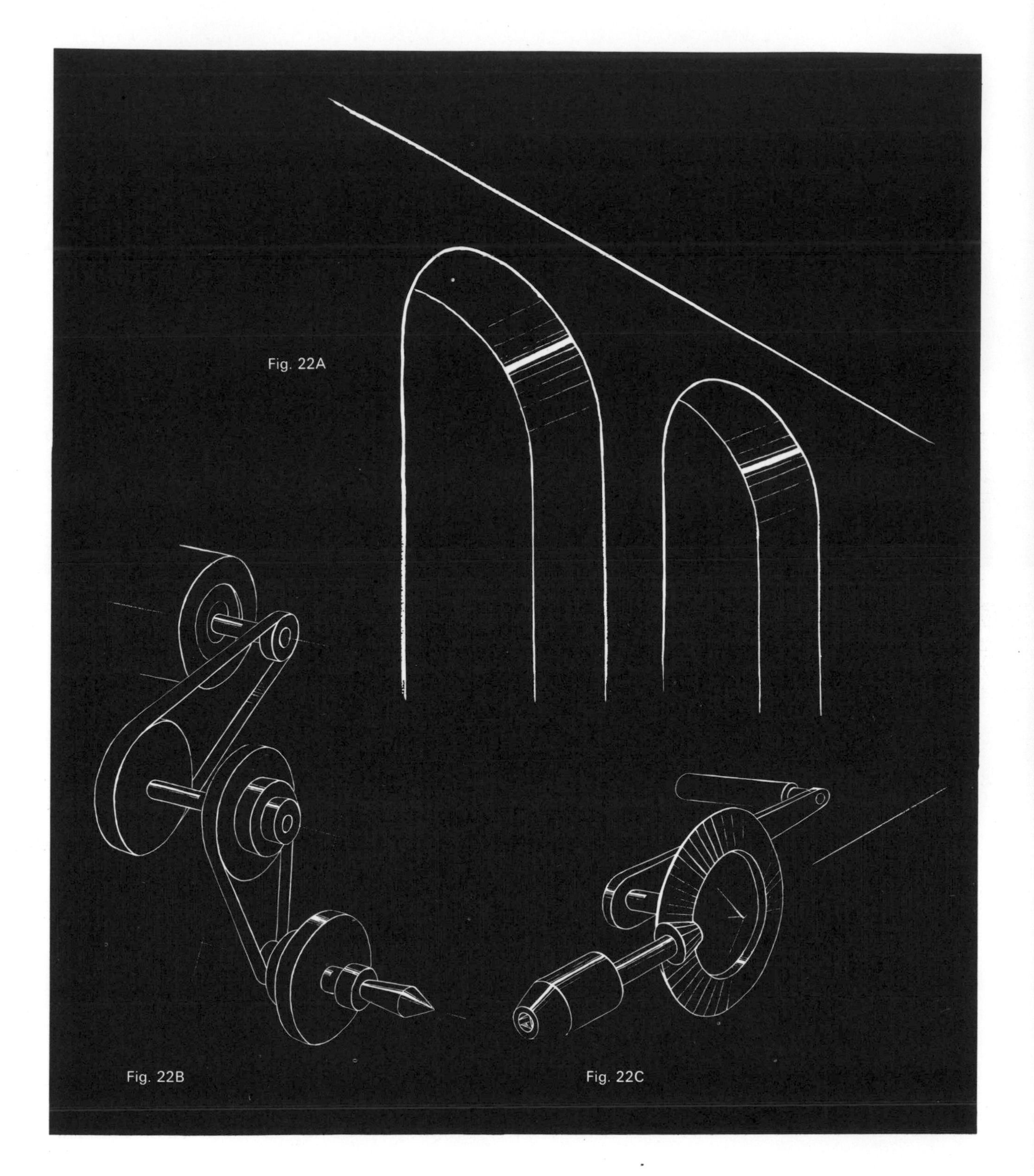
Fig. 22A

Fig. 22B

Fig. 22C

exercises for the horizontal cylinder

1 Practise drawing ellipses at right-angles to various lines drawn at perspective slopes, Fig. 19C.

2 Practise drawing complete cylinders, and be sure to use both left- and right-hand axes in your examples.

3 Draw the semi-cylinder, Fig. 21C.

4 Try a cylinder above the eye-level. If in doubt refer to the box, Fig. 18C, and Fig. 22A.

5 Try the system of pulleys in Fig. 22B. Set the axes of the shafts first, taking care with perspective parallelism, then draw the ellipses according to rule. The stepped pulleys are constructed from concentric ellipses.

6 Figure 22C shows the main parts of a hand drilling machine, with ellipses on both left- and right-hand axes. The direction of the teeth on the bevel gears is found by drawing in lightly the two cones with a common apex.

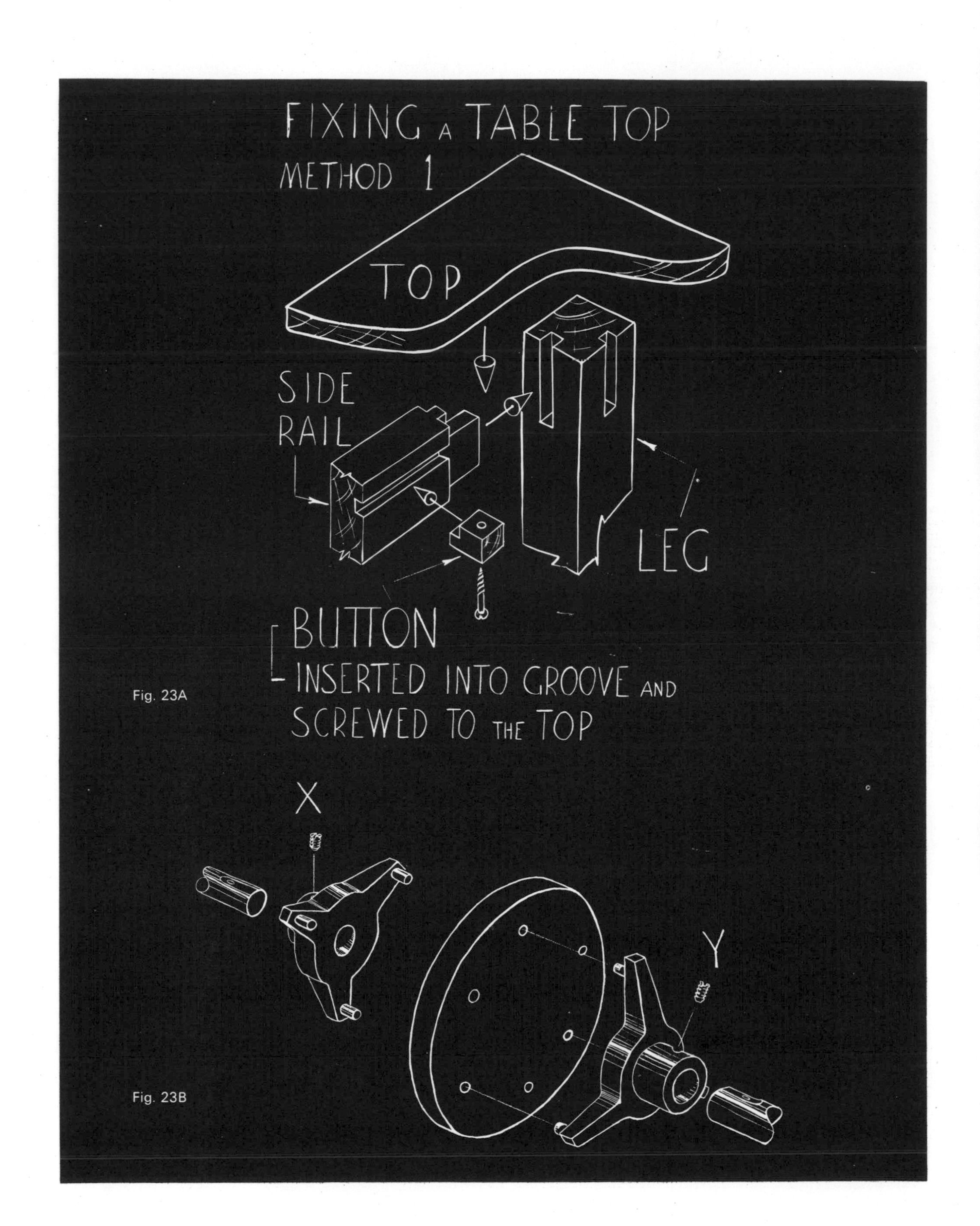

Fig. 23A

Fig. 23B

free-hand perspective drawing 5

EXPLODED VIEWS

1 Re-read Chalkwork 12 which applies to flat diagrams.

2 The vertical line and the two perspective horizontals which make the corner of the box, form a set of perspective axes. The set in Fig. 18A is below the eye-level and the set in Fig. 18C is above the eye-level. The component pieces of an object may be separated along one or more of these perspective axes. This type of drawing is termed an exploded view. The bridle joint, Fig. 18F, shows a single removal along the left-hand axis, and Fig. 23A is a more complicated drawing with explosion along all three axes. In Fig. 23B of a flexible coupling, the grub screw *X* is withdrawn along the vertical axis and the grub screw *Y* is withdrawn along an axis chosen at random.

3 The exploded view is extremely explicit, because the parts are transferred for clarity yet retain a sense of connection for understanding.

4 To construct an exploded drawing, start with the main item drawn in the desired position for viewing, then put in the other parts, retaining a perspective relationship, so that if one could squeeze the drawing along the perspective axes the parts would come together to form the whole.

5 It is wiser to keep to the horizontal and vertical axes until a good level of drawing skill has been achieved, before using random axes.

6 For practice, start by drawing a box with a loose lid lifted vertically.
Repeat for a cylindrical container.
Draw a match-box with the inner compartment withdrawn along a perspective axis.
Continue with examples from your field of teaching.

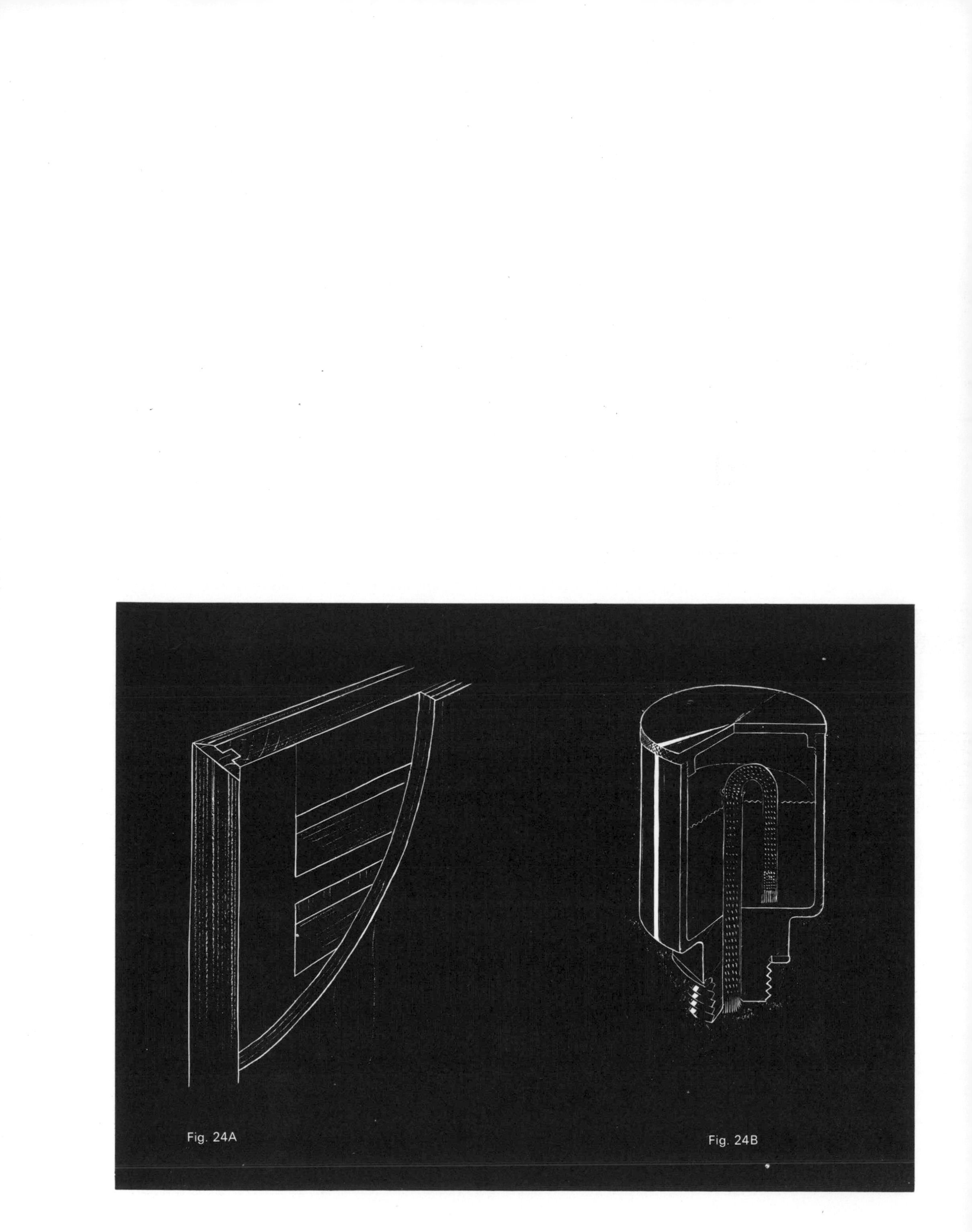

Fig. 24A

Fig. 24B

free-hand perspective drawing 6

BROKEN VIEWS

Because of the free-hand nature of this type of work, no conventional limitations are felt. The drawing may be sectioned, exploded or broken, i.e. a convenient piece of the object taken away to show covered detail.
Figure 13C shows a perspective half-section of a basin.
Figure 24A shows the plywood facing broken away from the corner of a framed, flush door.
Figure 24B shows a sector cut away from a wick-feed oil cup.

For practice:

1 Draw a triangular pyramid with the apex broken away.

2 Draw any perspective half-section through a hollow cube.

3 Draw a vertical cylinder with a sector removed.

4 Draw a horizontal cylinder with a sector removed.

5 Draw any perspective section through a hexagonal nut resting on one flat.

6 Continue with examples from your field of teaching.

0 A B C D
1
2
3
4
5
6
7 WAX
CRAYON

Fig. 25

enlargements for teaching charts

It is important that a classroom illustration is of sufficient size for easy viewing, and it is often necessary to produce a large teaching illustration from a small textbook illustration. A convenient method for enlargement is as follows:

1 Draw on the small illustration, or on a tracing of it, if the illustration cannot be marked, a square or a rectangular grid of pencil lines of convenient dimensions, e.g. $\frac{1}{2}'' \times \frac{1}{2}''$, $\frac{3}{4}'' \times \frac{3}{4}''$, $\frac{3}{4}'' \times 1\frac{1}{4}''$, etc.

2 Draw on a large piece of paper a similar grid of lines with the squares or rectangles enlarged to a convenient scale, e.g. $2'' \times 2''$, $1\frac{1}{2}'' \times 1\frac{1}{2}''$, $2\frac{1}{4}'' \times 3\frac{3}{4}''$, etc.

3 Mark on the outline of the small diagram a number of important reference points and then locate these points in identical positions on the enlarged grid.

4 Join up the new points to obtain the enlarged illustration. The number of reference points used will depend upon the shapes in the diagram, a curved line requiring more points than a straight line. Figure 25 shows the enlargement of a small drawing of a heraldic creature.

further practice examples

In attempting these exercises use light guide lines for placing, for shaping and for estimating proportions, and finish with clean and intense lines.

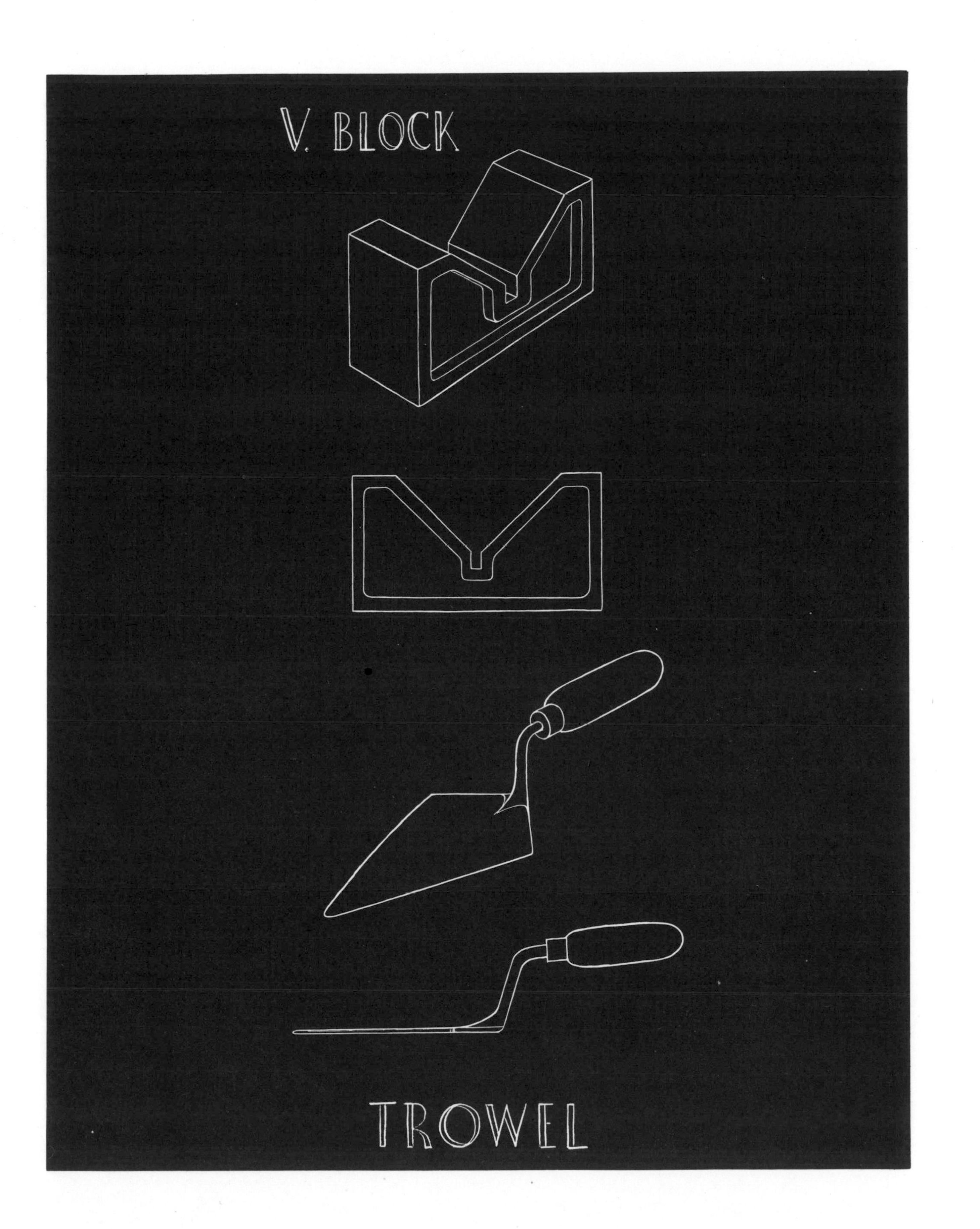
V. BLOCK
TROWEL

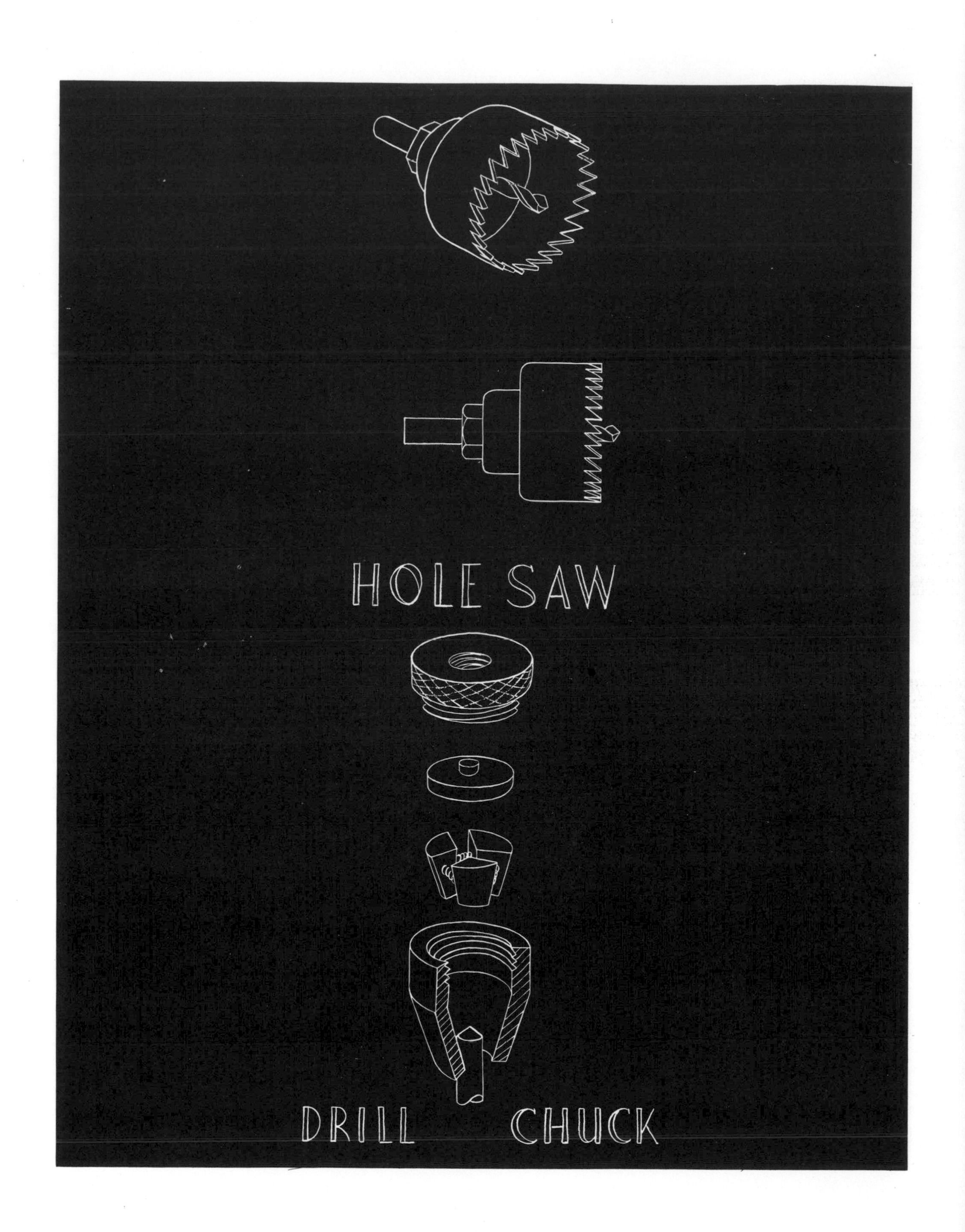
HOLE SAW
DRILL CHUCK

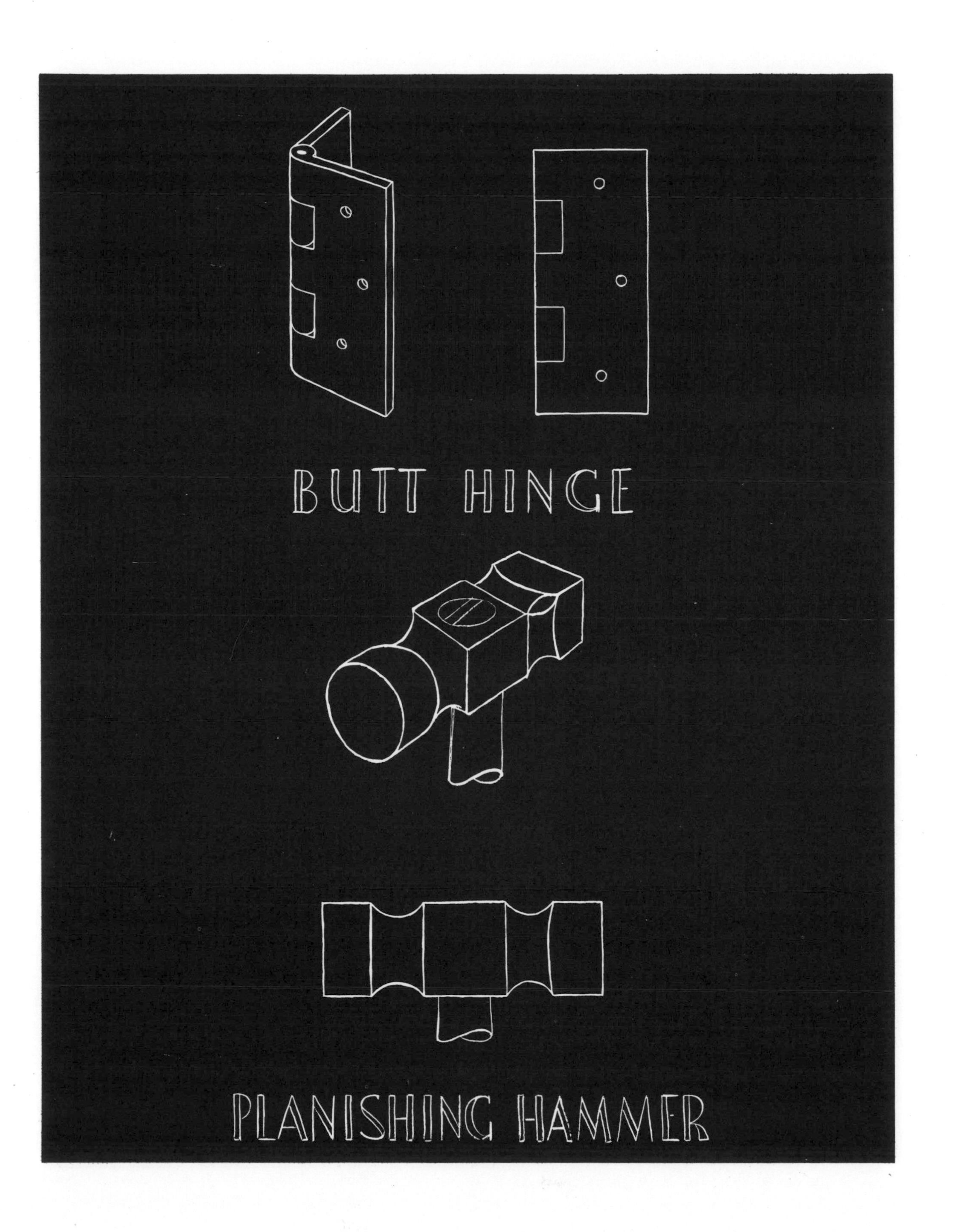
BUTT HINGE
PLANISHING HAMMER

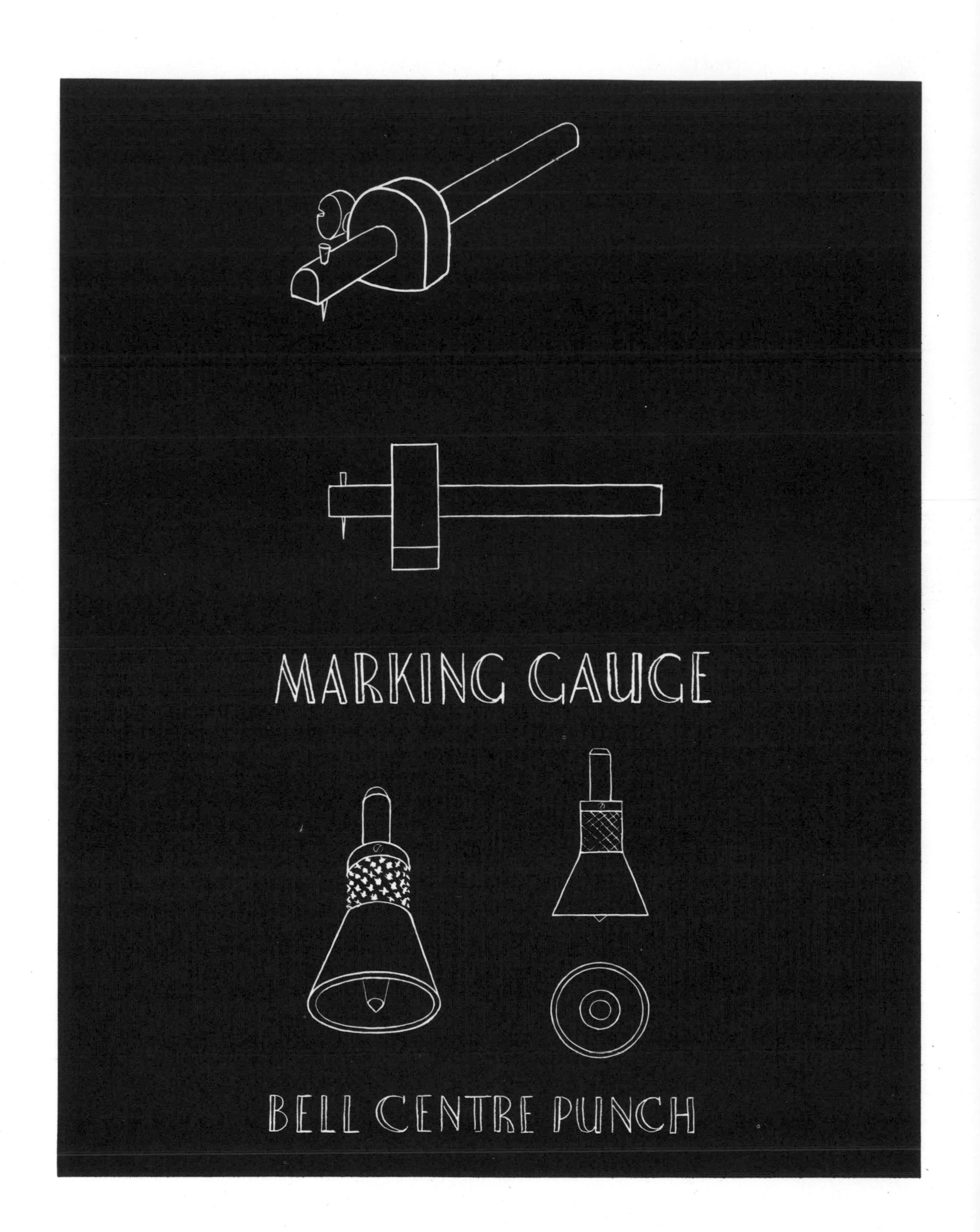
MARKING GAUGE
BELL CENTRE PUNCH